Seeds of
Perspective

Endorsements

Beth Grisham has written a must-read study for women! Beth has spent many years in the trenches, walking alongside of and loving women through some of their most difficult circumstances. Be empowered and encouraged by one of the best!

Steventhen Holland

Founder and President, Broken Not Dead Ministries

I have worked with Beth Grisham for over ten years as she has served as the executive director and I have served as the medical director at Shoals Sav a Life. I have had the privilege to come to know her and her heart for ministry. When one thinks of heart in a Scriptural sense, it includes the mind, the will, and the affections—what one thinks, does, and loves. This book will not only allow one to see Beth's heart and the hearts of the other contributors, but it will change yours as well.

Larry C. Stults, MD FACOG

It is evident in Beth's writing that she loves Jesus and has a huge heart for women. Over the years, she has developed great insight as she ministers to women on a daily basis. This may be just the book that could minister to a friend who is hurting or perhaps you know a small group of women who might benefit from reading it in a study group together. Don't miss out on this wonderful opportunity to grow in your personal relationship with Jesus and learn from the stories of these brave women who shared their journeys with their friend!

Peggy Hockenga

Assistant Professor, University of North Alabama,
Retired curriculum writer for Andy Andrews

Working with Beth was a true blessing. Beth was an inspiration to me as I shared my story of God's grace and love during a difficult time in our life. I'm forever thankful for Beth's ministry to women who are faced with difficult choices like I was. Her love and devotion to helping women and sharing God's word is a true testimony. I pray your heart will be touched as you read the words of these women and feel God speak to you and His love and grace overwhelmingly fill your heart.

Courtney Waldrop

Wife, mom of nine, TLC's *Sweet Home Sextuplets*

Seeds of Perspective

Planting Hope and Healing in the Baggage of Life

Beth Grisham

AMBASSADOR INTERNATIONAL
GREENVILLE, SOUTH CAROLINA & BELFAST, NORTHERN IRELAND

www.ambassador-international.com

Seeds of Perspective

Planting Hope and Healing in the Baggage of Life

©2022 by Beth Grisham
All rights reserved

ISBN: 978-1-64960-119-3
eISBN: 978-1-64960-169-8

Cover Design and Interior Typesetting by Christy Perry of Mercy's Hue

AMBASSADOR INTERNATIONAL
Emerald House
411 University Ridge, Suite B14
Greenville, SC 29601
United States
www.ambassador-international.com

AMBASSADOR BOOKS
The Mount
2 Woodstock Link
Belfast, BT6 8DD
Northern Ireland, United Kingdom
www.ambassadormedia.co.uk

The colophon is a trademark of Ambassador, a Christian publishing company.

Table of Contents

Introduction   9

CHAPTER 1
A Child of Addiction   17

CHAPTER 2
Abortion and Depression   27

CHAPTER 3
Infertility Issues   39

CHAPTER 4
Infidelity and Abortion   53

CHAPTER 5
Secret Struggles: A Birthmother's Perspective   63

CHAPTER 6
Marriage, Ministry and Porn   73

CHAPTER 7
Longing for Home   91

CHAPTER 8

Pure White 105

CHAPTER 9

He Gives and Takes Away 117

CHAPTER 10

Moments That Define Us 131

Conclusion 143

Questions for Group Discussion or Personal Reflection 145

About the Author 169

Introduction

I have known for some time that I would one day write a book. I simply had no idea that the process would include so many of my favorite people! It only makes the experience even more satisfying to take this journey with special friends. I say friends, but in truth, they are my sisters. I selected each one of them specifically because of the stories of their lives, and how I have seen God use those stories repeatedly to bless others. This book is filled with their humble, heartfelt, unashamedly candid accounts. Lest you think that their stories are unusual, let me assure you that many parts of them are more common than most might think. Which is exactly why I asked them to share their stories with you here. So that, if you are one who shares any similarities with the stories you are about to read, you will 1) know that you are not alone, and 2) hear that there is hope in your circumstance(s).

I have had the privilege of developing relationships with each of these women over the last twenty-five years as our paths have crossed through children, work, and general everyday activities. As we have journeyed, and in some instances served in different roles together, the roots of these friendships have grown deep, as they often do when you work side by side in the trenches of life's adventures. I work in a ministry setting where there is often the opportunity for me and others to sit with women who are in a crisis situation, to listen to their struggles, and then share the truth of God's love for them as we have experienced ourselves during our own crisis moments. Remembering and sharing awakens in each of us a deeper understanding of

God's promise to redeem our lives for His glory and His purposes, and to bring beauty from the ashes of our past. I can't tell you how often tears of healing have come from both our clients' eyes *and* ours, as we have experienced the grace and fulfillment of seeing God use us, and therefore pronouncing to our hearts anew that we have been completely redeemed. The healing that comes from those moments is beyond anything I can begin to explain. As I saw the healing that comes through sharing, I began to think of these friends and how their stories might be helpful to others, too.

When I approached each of these women with the idea of sharing their stories in a book, I did so very prayerfully. How *do* you walk up to someone and say, "Hey, I was really hoping that you would take your valuable time that none of us seem to have enough of and write some of the most intimate and personal details of your life, and let me compile them and then put in a book for the whole world to read."

While I knew they loved and trusted me, I wondered if I might be going one step too far in our friendship. But these ladies didn't run, which is obviously why they are the ones God placed on my heart to begin with. I'm *not* saying that they didn't look at me a little funny when I first broached the subject. I would say "shocked and a little nervous" describes their initial expressions accurately. One of them, an acquaintance of eighteen years, told me that as she read my initial letter explaining the project I had in mind, her heart began to beat faster, her neck turned red, and she even broke out in a sweat. With the many life moments that we've shared during those eighteen years, this was deeply personal for her. As she relayed her reaction to me, my heart was beating a little faster, too, and I gripped my phone with sweaty palms, worried that I might have offended her as my heart also hurt for the fact that this was a struggle for her. "Struggle" isn't nearly the right word. It took some gut wrenching, soul searching, stretching, and tears for these stories to go from the hearts of these ladies to being written on these pages. But after the initial look of terror began to fade from their eyes, their response, one by one, turned from nervousness to excitement. After taking some time to think and pray, they were willing, receptive, and humbled by the invitation to participate. They were certainly no more humbled than I was by the trust they were willing to place in me to walk them through the process of sharing their stories.

As you read these pages, someone may come to mind that you want to share them with. Maybe you will recognize in the story lines traces of the lives of people that you know. Or perhaps the person that will most identify is *you*. Maybe *you* have been longing to hear that you are not alone in your thoughts or in your experiences, and that a person exists that might understand your life and what you've been through. I hope that if that's you, you will have your own moment of revelation, and that in these pages you will find hope, joy, and even peace with your past.

You are not alone. I have come to understand that we all have a story. There is not one person that you will pass on the street, stand beside in the grocery line, see sleeping on a park bench or under a bridge, talk to at your child's next school or sporting event, or even sit beside on a church pew who doesn't have a story to tell. But the fact is, most of us don't tell our stories (or should I say won't?), and I'm not entirely sure why. Most of us are so familiar with our life stories that we don't realize how amazing they truly are. We tend to get so comfortable in our skin that we think that affairs, abortions, thoughts of rejection, anxiety, and depression are just normal, when in truth, they are not. Every affair is born from a reason, every abortion includes a story of loss, and feelings of rejection, anxiety, and depression all begin *some*where.

I think others remain silent because they don't think anyone would want to listen. Maybe they don't see that their story has value. Maybe they've been told to let their story die, pack up the details, and just move on. Or, maybe telling their story would also mean telling someone *else's* story that doesn't want their involvement to be told. And of course, there is always the possibility that the story is simply too hard to tell for fear of being judged if they just lay the truth out on the table. With those thoughts in mind, I suggested to my friends that these stories be told anonymously, possibly changing names and places to maintain the privacy of all identities. But anonymous or not, real names or disguised, the facts of the stories remain the same, because when it comes to being real, some things in life just can't be made to look pretty.

The most difficult part of writing for each of my friends seemed to be deciding what topic they would choose to address. When you consider that often a root issue will bear many more branch issues, you will understand the endless possibilities of the topics they might have had to pick from. It was like taking a hike through a field full of weeds in search of the one beautiful bloom that was ready to be picked and put on display—the one issue where truth and healing had blossomed to bring to the pages of this book the fragrance of the knowledge of Christ. To give clarity to their thoughts, I suggested that each one pray and consider the one specific topic God would have them to unpack by asking Him to give them one word.

In a podcast, one of my favorite teachers mentioned having a friend that seeks a new "God word" each year, a focus word of sorts. He said that once during an outing together, his friend asked him what his word was for the year, and that much to his chagrin, he could only report that he didn't have one. So, his friend suggested a word. After parting ways and giving the word some thought, he said that he didn't feel settled that the suggested word was the correct word for him. A short time later this same friend again asked this preacher if he had found his word, to which he replied that he thought his friend had *given* him a word. The friend responded quickly to clarify that the word wasn't meant to *be* his word but was simply meant as a *suggestion* to get the process started. He went on to say that he *couldn't* give him his word—only God could. Now, with a better understanding of the concept, this preacher came to the conclusion that the word his friend had suggested was intended to draw something out of him—his word—that was already in him, and he eventually came up with the word that God wanted to speak personally to him.

The words my friends chose to focus on are intended to help you find your word as well. You may already have a word, a word that comes to your thoughts on a regular basis. Like the preacher I mentioned, it may even be a word that was assigned to you by a friend. But I would challenge you, just as I challenged my friends, to lay aside every word man has spoken over you and to ask God Himself to give you a word that He might want to use to unpack some truth for you.

I like the analogy of unpacking, because truly, I think we all have baggage that we carry around. We've locked the suitcase up tight and packed the contents away in the back corner of the closet. But maybe it's finally time to pull out the old suitcase from journeys taken long ago and reopen our baggage, pulling the usable things out and washing the dirty laundry in the Living Water so that we can pronounce it washed and clean, processed, and ready to be neatly and *properly* put in its place. Not wadded up, tucked under a rug, or hidden under the covers with the stink still in it, but washed, sorted, sized, and put away. The best part is, when you handle the things in your baggage this way, you will be able to get rid of what doesn't fit you anymore. Isn't that a wonderful thought?

As the mother of five daughters and one son, this makes me think of the closet clean outs that happened every spring and fall as the seasons changed while my children were growing up. The worn and stained articles, the items that no longer fit, or the once trendy items were removed, replaced with clothing that fit more appropriately. That is what I hope you will do, too. I hope that you will recognize the season that you are currently in, size things up, and after properly sorting through the contents of your bag, remove the stained, the out of season, and the "no longer you" items that you once wore and have been hanging onto and dragging around, and still trying to fit into.

As I mentioned earlier, my role was to compile these stories and to bring the variety of individual stories together to house inside of one book cover. Rather than rewrite them all to sound more uniform as some suggested I should, I attempted to leave each story written as close as possible to the final version that was submitted by each writer so that the uniqueness of each woman would remain intact. And hopefully, you, the reader, might identify more readily with the heart and experience of the original writer.

We all have friends that might need us to be more knowledgeable and understanding of similar things that they may have walked through, so I would suggest reading each chapter even if one might seem not to fit your circumstance.

In Luke chapter 2, as the shepherds came to see the baby Jesus and then left to spread the wonderful news of all that they had been told about Him, Mary's response was to take in the things that she saw and heard and to treasure all of these things up and ponder them in her heart. I absolutely love this thought of "pondering" the things that God speaks. To help you ponder, I have included at the end of each chapter some concepts and topics that stood out to me as I read through each of these stories. Go deeper in your understanding of each account by taking time to work through the discussion material either on your own or in a group study. I truly believe that each of these experiences has a nugget included for each reader to find and take away.

It is my greatest joy and pleasure to introduce and share my friends with you. They are more priceless than rubies, and they are such brave souls. Together we have prayed for you as you take in the parts of their journeys they have humbly shared. Let me remind you that these stories were bought with the blood of Christ in the moment that each one gave her life to Him, just as in that moment He also received the best and most wonderful qualities they each possess. Just in case there is any doubt, or any woman reading this who still wonders, Jesus Christ has paid the price for your stories, too. All you must do is share them with Him, believe He died to redeem them, and confess Him as the Lord of your life. (I'll share more about that later.) We are praying that either you have or will experience that truth, and so, the stories have been shared as a testimony to His faithfulness. May God bless your reading of each story and may the rest of your life be a story that reveals Him to others.

Beth Grisham

CHAPTER 1

A Child of Addiction

I have dealt with addiction in some way for my entire life. Experts say that addiction is something that doesn't just affect the addict, but everyone around them, too. Unfortunately, I know just how true that statement is. My father was an addict. He was addicted to alcohol and prescription drugs, opioids specifically. My parents divorced because of my father's addiction when I was five years old and my brother was six. Six years later, when my brother was twelve and I was eleven, my mom married my stepfather who was also an addict. His drug of choice was crack cocaine. I use the term "was" an addict for these two men in my life because they both are now free of their addictions, although they have very different stories with very different endings.

Between my father and stepfather my middle school and high school days were often spent in chaos. I identify my middle school years as the time in my life when my stepdad was the main source of chaos, and my high school years as the time that my dad took over that role. As if middle school years aren't stressful enough for a kid with the hormones and body changes taking place, this was when my mom decided to remarry. If I could describe the relationship of my mom and my stepdad as anything, it would be a roller-coaster ride full of ups and downs, highs and lows. In the beginning things were great. Of course, throwing a stepparent into the mix when you have two middle school-aged kids comes with its challenges, but for the most part things were good. My stepdad and I had a good relationship from the very beginning, and he seemed like a great guy. My mom was happy, and I was enjoying having a somewhat normal two parent home, but then things really began to change.

My mom and stepdad started fighting regularly, but I didn't think much of it until he began not coming home for a few days or even a week at a time. I remember discussing it with my brother and trying to figure out what was really going on. Although we were just kids, we still knew that something wasn't right and that there was more to the situation than we were being told. After overhearing their fights from another room (when he came home) and doing our best to listen in on phone conversations, we began to figure things out. It appeared that my stepdad had a drug problem, and during those times that he wasn't coming home, he was somewhere getting high.

Over the next couple of years my stepdad's pattern was to get high for a while, go to rehab, come home, stay sober for a while, then start getting high again, and then back to rehab he would go. I always kind of liked it when he would go to rehab because things were a lot more peaceful around our house. In the middle of all the chaos, my mom got pregnant and had my baby brother. I was so upset when I found out that I wasn't going to be the baby of the family anymore, but when my baby brother was born, he immediately became my little sidekick. He was his Sissy's baby from day one, and he still is to this day. By the time my baby brother was a few months old my stepdad was using again. Thankfully, the family finally told him enough was enough and that something had to change. He went to rehab for the last time.

When he left, I didn't care if I ever saw him again, and to be honest, I secretly wished my mom would leave him. I thought that this was going to be just like every other time he went to rehab, and that before long he would go right back to getting high. I am glad to say that I was wrong. God radically changed his life in his last rehab, and my stepdad never went back to using drugs. Today, my stepdad is the director of a faith-based life recovery program for people who are struggling with addiction, and he also pastors a church. So, my stepdad *was* an addict, but he allowed God to break the chains of addiction from his life, and he can now help others who are going through the same thing.

Now for my dad's story. My father had always been an alcoholic. I think "functioning alcoholic" is a good way to describe him. I never doubted that he loved me. After my parents' divorce, he always took care of me and my brother when we went to his house. He was never mean or violent toward us, and he always had a good job. I hated the fact that he drank, because even though he wasn't a mean drunk, I still didn't like the way he acted while he was drinking. Most of the time he would drink until he would pass out, so he was often passed out in his recliner when we went to visit. My brother and I watched a lot of television and ordered a lot of pizza while we were there. All through middle school when everything was going on with my stepdad, Daddy's drinking continued. But it was no more than usual, and by this point in my life I had become numb to it, resigning myself to the fact that this was just something he was going to do. He always thought that what he did was so much better than my stepdad because in his eyes he was just drinking, not smoking crack. I had no idea that by the time I entered high school unfortunate events to come would turn my once "functioning alcoholic" dad into a full-blown drug addict right before my eyes.

One night while my dad was driving home from work, he was involved in a horrible car accident. He fell asleep while driving and sustained a substantial back injury. Several surgeries were required to correct the damage, and they became the catalyst that caused him to take a turn for the worse in his addiction. My dad was prescribed several different medications to manage his pain as most patients are after surgery. He was unable to return to work after the wreck, so he was home bound most of the time. As a result, he became severely depressed and was prescribed even more medication to cope with that as well. My dad was already addicted to alcohol and adding addictive pain medications to the mix didn't help matters at all.

In the weeks, months, and years to follow, my Daddy's days were consumed with drowning his pain in a bottle of whiskey and a handful of pills. He would use his depression and his physical pain as excuses to justify his addictions. Every other weekend came, and my brother and I went to spend our weekend with him, but we were uncertain by this point of what kind of state we would find him in. I could always tell as soon as I saw him how the weekend was going to go. Sometimes we would get there on Friday afternoon and he would be sober. "Hey, baby girl," he would say from his recliner when I walked in, and that was like Christmas morning for me. Sometimes I would be so happy that I would crawl up and sit in his lap like I was five years old again and just hug him. I didn't care that I was a teenager, because for a little while I got to spend time with the real version of my daddy that I so desperately missed and longed for, the daddy who was funny, loving, and so generous that he would give you the shirt off of his back if he knew you needed it. We would sit and talk for hours, maybe go out to eat, or my brother would play his guitar, and we would all sit around and sing every song we could remember. Those were the best days, and I took full advantage of them whenever they happened. Other times, we would walk in to find him passed out on the couch, his recliner, or even on the floor. Sometimes he would be so high that he could barely hold his eyes open from the pills he had taken. I remember begging him to stop and to choose me; not the pills or the alcohol, but *ME*! I never understood why he just wouldn't stop, why he wouldn't just flush those pills and pour out that whiskey and choose my brother and me. We needed him. I was a desperate, broken teenage girl that needed my daddy. I offered to help him get into rehab so many times, but he would never accept my help. He always defaulted to his back pain and depression, saying that he had to take the pills.

For a couple of months at a time, he would "sober up." He would still take his medicine, but not enough to get high. During those times he was present physically, but not totally there emotionally. Many weekends came and went where my dad was so intoxicated between the mixture of alcohol and pills that he wouldn't even know that my brother and I had been there the entire weekend. This became the new normal in my relationship with my dad throughout my teenage years. I always knew that he couldn't continue to live doing the things that he was doing. He had lived through overdoses and suicide attempts, and I didn't want to see anything happen to him.

One summer day in July, when I was nineteen, the call came from the police that I will never forget. "Something has happened, and you need to come to your daddy's house right away." I honestly thought that he had gotten high and fallen and hurt himself, or that maybe he did something stupid like getting in a fight with a neighbor. When I got to my dad's house, my worst nightmare became a reality. Police were everywhere, and fire trucks and ambulances lined the street. I'll never forget the officer coming up to me and telling me that my father had died. They didn't even have to tell me that it was from an overdose. I already knew. I remember just dropping to my knees in the middle of the street and crying. For a few minutes it was like everything was a blur going on around me while I was trying to process the news that I had just received. Even though I had played this scenario out in my head so many times, I wasn't prepared for this. Losing a parent when you are so young, especially to drugs, is an excruciating pain that you can't fathom until you've lived it. My dad also "was" an addict, and unfortunately his addiction eventually ended his life.

Even with all the chaos that I lived through as a child and a teenager, my relationship with God has always been a constant. I thank my mom for that. She always made sure that we were in church no matter what was happening in our lives, and that we understood that serving and honoring God was the most important thing. I was saved at church camp when I was ten years old. I can remember as a little girl listening to worship music on a cassette tape and hanging Bible verses on the walls of my bedroom. Later I'd take my Bible to sleepovers in middle school. I knew that God could change my daddy's life if he would let him, because if he would do it for my stepdad, he would do it for my daddy, too. Sometimes when he was high and passed out on the couch, I would pray over him asking God to deliver my daddy from his addiction. I knew even before my dad died that I wanted to help people who were affected by drug addiction one day. When he was alive, especially during those times where he would sober up for a couple of months at a time, he would always tell me, "Baby girl, the world needs people like you, and you're going to help a lot of people one day."

One night following my dad's death, as I was listening to the song "How He Loves" by David Crowder, God spoke to me through a part of a verse in that song and forever changed my view on how I saw my life up until this point. The verse talks about "afflictions eclipsed by glory." It made me realize more than ever that no matter what I had gone through, my afflictions in life were allowed by God to be used for His glory. I knew that the struggles in my daddy's life and everything we went through with my stepdad's addictions was not in vain.

At the time my dad died, I was taking basic classes at a local community college, not really knowing where I was going or what I was going to do after that. I had always known that whatever career path I chose I wanted to help people, so I decided there was no better group of people to help than those who were going through the same things that I had been through. I finished college and obtained a degree in Substance Abuse Counseling that can be used not only to help individuals who are struggling with addiction, but also to support the loved ones of people who are struggling with addiction as well.

Being a Christian doesn't make you immune to being affected negatively by the things that happen in your life, and I can't say that I haven't had my fair share of struggles along the way. Just like anyone else, there have been times in my life when my relationship with God was stronger than at other times, but I have always known that He is the answer. Have there been times when I questioned God as to why my dad had to be a drug addict? Yes, many times. Have I ever questioned God about why my mom had to financially struggle so much when we were growing up? You better believe it. Have I asked God why I couldn't have just had a "normal" life? More times than I can count. I was taught in church that we are supposed to "Consider it pure joy, my brothers and sisters, whenever you face trials of many kinds" (James 1:2). But let's be real. It has been hard to find joy in most of the circumstances I have been in.

I think one of the biggest ways that I was affected emotionally by the addiction-riddled relationships with my dad and stepdad was that I always felt insecure. A father is supposed to be someone that you feel safe and secure with, your provider, your protector; but there was never any real security with the two men in my life who were supposed to be that for me. Our relationships could be great one day and then in shambles the next. Since there was never any consistent security, I always tried to fill that void with a relationship with another man. For as long as I can remember I always had a boyfriend. From the time I was fourteen until I got married at twenty-one there were very few days that I was single. I would stay in a relationship for a year or two then move right into another one a few months later. My heart ached for stability and security because I had not experienced that type of relationship with a male in my entire life.

When I was twenty years old, I started dating a man who was ten years older than me. I remember thinking that this guy was completely different than anyone that I had ever dated, so it would be a good change for me. The first thing that drew me to him was that he had a great job where he made good money. Insecurity about money has always been a huge issue for me. My dad stopped paying my mom child support after he had the accident and was unable to go back to work. That meant that my mother was primarily left to take care of our financial needs on her own. I remember her crying on days when money was tight, and she didn't know how she was going to pay the bills. But somehow, she always made it work. As a result, I always told myself that I wanted to be financially stable, and because this new man in my life had a good income, I would not have to worry about money if I did marry him.

He was a Christian, which was also a good thing, and he even played the guitar and sang at church. We got along well, and we never fought like I had always seen my parents do. His parents had been married for fifty years, and they seemed great, too. He was literally the definition of security for me. We didn't date very long before getting engaged, and we were married less than a year later. Everything was great for a while, and I was certain that I had found the security in this relationship that I had always longed for. We led worship at our church, we were able to take vacations every year, we always had plenty of money, we lived in a nice home, we both drove nice vehicles, and to the world we looked like a perfect couple. However, our life was far from perfect. After four years of marriage, some bad decisions on his part, and one baby later, our marriage ended in divorce. Yes, you heard me correctly: the worship leader and his wife who was also the pastor's daughter got divorced.

I always told myself that I would never get divorced after having lived with parents who were divorced, and I never dreamed that my ex-husband and I would be in the process of finalizing our divorce before our son's first birthday. But regardless of what I thought, that's where we were. I learned more than ever that those situations that you declare will "never happen to me" can happen, no matter how hard you try to avoid them. I stayed in my marriage for a long time, turning a blind eye to things that I knew were taking place out of my need for security. I thought that I would never be able to make it on my own. I didn't want my family, friends, and church to know that my marriage was in shambles. But I also knew that I didn't want to stay in a marriage tainted with infidelity for the rest of my life, so I finally filed for divorce. I felt like a complete failure, and I was more insecure than ever at this point in my life. "Am I really going to get a divorce? How am I ever going to make it financially on my own? Can I really make it as a single mom? Will I be able to give my son the life that he deserves? What are people going to think of me? What will the church think of me?" These are all questions that I asked myself daily. I knew God hated divorce. That's like, a *big* sin, right? I still showed up at church every Sunday and Wednesday with a smile on my face and tried to act like I was fine, but I was a complete mess.

I allowed my mind to be tortured by the lies of Satan for months. Then the last day of the year came, and just like every other New Year's Eve I was thinking about all that had taken place the past year. This time I thought about how different my life looked on the last day of the year from the first day. I had gone through a divorce, moved out of my home and into an apartment, my son was a year old, and I was now a single mom. I was watching my son play in the living room floor of the apartment and tears began to rush down my face as I sat there watching him. I felt like I had failed as his mother in so many ways in the first year of his life, but he didn't seem to have a care in the world. He was just happy to play with his mommy. He didn't see me as a failure. He saw me as his provider, his comforter, and his safe place to run to. The Lord was able to minister to me in that moment and reminded me that just as my son didn't see me as a failure, neither did He. The scripture in Romans 8:35-39 came to my mind. It says, "Who shall separate us from the love of Christ? Shall trouble or hardship or persecution or famine or nakedness or danger or sword? As it is written: 'For your sake we face death all day long; we are considered as sheep to be slaughtered.' No, in all these things we are more than conquerors through him who loved us. For I am convinced that neither death nor life, neither angels nor demons, neither the present nor the future, nor any powers, neither height nor depth, nor anything else in all creation, will be able to separate us from the love of God that is in Christ Jesus our Lord."

I had been through so much change that year facing tribulation, distress, and persecution. I thought I would never be loved again. I even questioned if God could still love me anymore. I carried so much guilt, shame and depression because I was divorced from my husband. I saw myself as "the divorced girl." I thought that I didn't deserve happiness, and I felt like I walked around with a t-shirt on every day that had the word "DIVORCED" written across the front of it for the world to see and judge. The truth was that I was the only one that woke up and put on that "DIVORCED" shirt in my mind every day. God had been with me every step of the way, loving me through every situation that I had been in. He reminded me who I was that day: I was more than a conqueror through Him Who loves me. He reminded me that just as I was my son's provider, his comforter, and his safe place to run to, God still wanted to be those things for me. With Him, nothing had changed. I use the word "reminded" to encourage you, too, because sometimes even the best Christians can get so caught up in the troubles that this world brings that they need a reminder from God of who they are in Him.

Today, I am freer than I have ever been. I've had to learn to let go of the picture of what I thought my life should look like and to learn to find joy in the life I am living. I am doing my best to find my security in God and not in a relationship with a man, and I have realized that I will never be secure in any relationship or any area of my life until that happens. I have had to forgive myself for mistakes I have made along the way, and to learn to love myself again. My son is the absolute best gift that God has ever given to me and being a good mom to him is my top priority. I know that God has amazing things in store for my life, and through the courage and strength that He gives to me, I am looking forward to the next steps in my journey with Him.

CHAPTER 2

Abortion and Depression

When trouble comes, count it all joy. This teaching is found in James 1:2 and is something I never understood in my earlier years. It was only after I chose a personal relationship with Jesus Christ, and even more specifically in the last few years, that I have actualized this as a life verse in my spirit. I am now sixty-five. Woe is me that it took me this long. I understand our walk is and should be a persistent path of progress toward our sanctification, but my progress has been very slow. I've always envied those who come to understand at an early age who Jesus is and therefore avoid choosing self-destructive paths toward pain and sorrow. Most of my life trials have been consequences of my sins against God. Distracted and enticed, I worshipped myself, others, and many things of this world. I did not truly understand about obeying or worshipping God, nor did I want to, and I paid a steep price.

I was raised in a Christian home where I occasionally went to church with my parents, but God was never talked about in our daily life. My grandmother was the one who passed down her Christian legacy to me, and I thank God for her influence on my faith. She taught me about Jesus as we sat under a giant maple tree in her front yard and although it took time to bear fruit in my life, her teaching took root. I accepted Christ as my Savior and was baptized when I was in the eighth grade, but because I never learned about having a close personal relationship with God, my faith never really influenced how I lived my life.

I became somewhat rebellious my junior year in high school. My friends and I weren't *bad* girls. We made decent grades, we were popular, and we never got into any serious trouble. We drank some even though we were underage, but we never got caught. Drinking alcohol and partying eventually lead to smoking marijuana. My inhibitions and common sense would fly right out of the door when I drank or smoked pot. I became sexually active with my boyfriend with no thought about it being right or wrong, potentially deadly, or leading to life-altering consequences. My parents explained the facts of life, but just as their sharing of faith matters fell short, so did their discussion of sexual issues. There was not much dialogue about discipline, life direction, or God's commandments either, for that matter.

Growing up as an only child, I never saw my parents argue or fight. Having no siblings, I never learned to stand up for myself, nor did I learn how to handle confrontation or how to manage conflict resolution. I knew my parents loved me, but they didn't verbally express their love very often or show much affection through physical gestures. There were few words of affirmation, especially from my mother. I think all of this factored into why I became a gullible, vulnerable teenager with low self-esteem, who didn't know who I was and had no understanding of my self-worth. That state of mind was the perfect mix for creating the perfect storm in a young life. However, I don't want you to think that I see myself as a victim, because in all fairness, my past problems are due to my own choices and actions.

In the spring of my junior year of high school I became pregnant. I never told my parents, and there was never any discussion from anyone about my options. I had a problem and my boyfriend and I simply needed to fix it. With my consent, my boyfriend sought help from his sister who was much older, and arrangements were made for me to fly to New York City for an abortion. In 1971 that was the only place to go for a *safe* and legal abortion. I'm not sure how, but my boyfriend obtained the money to pay for everything. I look back now and I realize that it was much too easy. My boyfriend took me to the airport, and I boarded the plane bound for New York City. The clinic driver met me when I landed and drove me and another woman to the clinic. After the procedure was performed, he drove us both back to the airport where we boarded the plane and ended up sitting next to each other during the flight. I noticed that she appeared to be very despondent, and she ordered a drink. I, on the other hand, felt very relieved and glad that it was over. My problem was fixed, and I suffered no complications. I was back at home that evening as if nothing had ever happened. My parents thought that I had been at the lake all day with my friends. *Wow, what a breeze that was!* I thought. I was only seventeen. My parents never knew, and I was not going to tell them. My boyfriend and I eventually broke up, and I never spoke about the abortion again to anyone until about thirty years later.

After I healed from the procedure, I went to a local Planned Parenthood and they started me on birth control. I continued to view sex outside of marriage as being okay if I was "in love" with the guy, but I did not think it was okay to have one-night stands, nor did I believe in "free love" as many in that era did. While in college, I married a man who liked to party, drink alcohol, and smoke pot. He was fun and it didn't matter to me that he wasn't a Christian. We married and before long had a son together, but my husband cheated on me regularly, and I finally filed for divorce due to adultery. I stopped partying after my son was born, and I worked hard to graduate college and become a nurse. After a few years passed, I started dating again. I thought my son needed a stepdad who would be a good role model, so I remarried two years later to a man who had a farm and horses. Why? Because I love horses! Again, it didn't matter to me that he wasn't a Christian: he had *horses*! I know you are thinking I was so shallow, but I honestly thought that I was in love. I realized all too late that I was in love with the farm and the horses, but not the man I married.

We tried to have a baby but were unable to conceive due to scarring in my pelvis from an STD I had contracted from my ex-husband as a result of his multiple affairs. We tried in vitro fertilization, which resulted in five living embryos. Three were implanted, but I miscarried all three. We still had two embryos that we paid to keep frozen at the fertility clinic. After a few years, this husband, too, was unfaithful, and once again I divorced. He was a harsh stepfather to my son, so it was probably the best thing for him as well. In the divorce my ex would not agree to allow our remaining two embryos to be adopted out. I reluctantly allowed him to convince me to let the embryos thaw and be disposed of at the clinic. *They weren't really babies yet,* I thought. But in my heart, I knew that I allowed those two babies to die. I never spoke about it again to anyone.

Several years after that divorce, I remarried again. Even with my other failed marriages, I had always wanted to be married, but I wanted a *good* marriage. This time it was important to me that he was a Christian. My husband and I were married after dating long distance for a couple of years, and I moved to the state where he lived. I began going to church and learning about a personal relationship with Jesus Christ. I also began volunteering at a local crisis pregnancy center, because at this point in my life, I had begun to feel badly about my abortion all those years ago. Gone were the feelings of relief I had felt immediately following the procedure now that I was no longer seventeen and worried about facing my mom and dad. I felt remorse, and I wanted to help others not to make the same mistake I made. I also decided that God's plan for sex within the confines of marriage was truly the way it should be. For a long time, I thought I knew better than God about how to live my life, and I made my own choices. But I could now attest that His plan truly was best. I realized that if I had obeyed God in my early adult life, I might have avoided a tremendous amount of heartache.

I thought I was a happy person, but I struggled with pesky bouts of recurring, mild depression. After much prayer, I felt God revealing to me that I was battling depression because I was subconsciously hearing the cries of my three children that I had murdered. Their cries became more haunting and real to me with each passing day. God showed me that I had never confessed my sins of murder. Me, a murderer? How could I have done that? I realized that my choices from all those years ago were the source of my depression. To me, the word abortion meant that I took care of my *problem.* I had never made the correlation between the words, *abortion* and *murder.* It was too painful to admit the truth, to call my actions out for what they really were by admitting I had committed murder—and it was premeditated at that. Many of us who have had an abortion can't bring ourselves to face this truth. If we do, then we begin to condemn ourselves by believing God would surely never forgive us since we are struggling so to even forgive ourselves. Besides confronting these emotions, I felt angry toward everyone who had been a part of the situation: myself, my boyfriend, society in general at that time, and my parents whom I couldn't talk with openly.

I had also suppressed the need to grieve the loss of my children. I believe a woman has a subconscious need to grieve when her child dies, no matter how the death occurs. In cases like mine, one of the most important things needed to begin the healing process is to repent for taking the life of your child. For as long as the choices that we make remain unfaced and tucked away in the secret places of our hearts, we will suffer in mind, body, and spirit. Subconscious suffering, as well as emotional and spiritual damage, will continue to take place until a person finally repents and allows herself to grieve the sinful actions committed against God, as well as the life of the child that was killed.

God revealed to me that ever since those life changing decisions had been made all the way back in my high school years, I had subconsciously been putting all of my painful experiences, heartbreaks, broken promises, dreams, and sins—which I now acknowledged as murder, anger, guilt, unforgiveness, bitterness, and pride—into little boxes with their appropriate labels. My mind told me that I needed to store these things somewhere safe, so subconsciously

I had excavated a "basement" deep in my soul, placing them where no one, not even God, could see them—or so I thought! There was a dimly lit staircase that I could easily navigate my way down in my mind from my conscious state that led to a door below that was always locked, but I had the key to get inside. Behind the locked door my boxes had safe harbor from my conscious common sense, mindful reasoning, confession, and repentance. They were never to be opened, *never*, except by me, and *only* me. They were mine, containing things that I needed to hang on to in case I needed them for moments of self-pity in which I often relished. *Poor pitiful me*, I thought. I deserved so much better.

In my mind, God took me by the hand and led me down the stairway. As we descended into the darkness, we entered a dimly lit room where I saw three boxes. They sat there, tightly wrapped, each labeled *My Child*. I knew exactly what the boxes meant, and I was willing to admit what I had done. As I cried out in confession and repentance for murder, He lovingly listened and forgave me. After that revelation I joined a support group at the pregnancy resource center where I volunteered and took part in a Bible study called *Forgiven and Set Free*[1]. I was relieved to know that I was not the only one going through this experience. The participants then attended a memorial service for our children. Although I cried uncontrollably the entire time, I felt a sense of relief that I was finally able to grieve the loss of my children. God revealed to me that He had them safe with Him in heaven and that I will know them one day. I also asked the Holy Spirit to do a full examination of my mind, body, and spirit. His exam light was brilliant, His stethoscope could hear the deepest moaning of my heart, and His touch was gentle. But still, He knew I hadn't opened any of my other boxes.

Several years later, a very stressful time in my marriage brought me to my knees in many hours of prayer. As I sought His wisdom and guidance, He

---

1   Cochrane, Linda. *Forgiven and Set Free: A Post-Abortion Bible Study for Women* (United States: Baker Publishing Group, 2015).

again reminded me that I had several more boxes to deal with in the basement. I had added rooms there, but the boxes weren't big enough to hold all my issues and unconfessed sins that I had accumulated over the years.

In my mind, He allowed me to see a beautiful room furnished with my past innocent expectations, the broken promises, and plans that had been taken from me. I had decorated the walls with beautiful paintings of my suppressed anger and beautiful vases that held my anger and bitterness. A golden chest was filled with my guilt of covetousness. Huge mirrors of my hopes and dreams had been shattered with glass pieces lying on the floor waiting to cut deep. The rugs were beautiful, but the designs held colorful images of my confusing nightmares.

That room led into a great hall of depression and despair. A beautiful chandelier hung from the ceiling to illuminate my past. I had placed a beautiful chair in this room, upholstered in a gorgeous tapestry woven with golden threads of self-pity and pride. I deserved it! I could go sit there when I was mad or hurt and remember all the sorrows I had endured in my past. I was not going to forgive those who had hurt me! I found a sense of security and comfort sitting there, thinking that I would never be hurt again. I looked around and noticed that I had also built an altar in this grand room. It was for many of my self-made idols. Of course, *I* was my favorite, but pride, anger, guilt for other things in my life, and unforgiveness were very high on the platform. From my chair—or should I say throne—I could sit and worship my idols in peace and quiet. It was just perfect! I was secure there in my sinfulness, queen of my universe, and I dictated what took place there. I never allowed God to come into that place.

This is where I was sitting when I felt something like an earthquake. I was knocked off my beautiful throne. When I regained my balance, I saw that my rooms had become like a jail. I was trapped in a dark, cold, musty cell, confused, but when I tried to escape, the doors were locked. I could not get out. I couldn't find the key this time, even though I did everything I knew to do. I called my friends for their advice, read books, and even watched a few sermons, but with no luck. I had problems, and I didn't know how to fix them. After a while, I got used to being there and being there became my *normal*. I had been miserably trapped for a while in the cage that I had built all by myself and decorated without even realizing it.

After several weeks, I was at the end. I stopped fighting and instead started asking Jesus to show me what He wanted me to do and what His will was for my life. I wanted what was normal in His kingdom rather than my universe I had built. I didn't need luck or anything else I had previously tried to use to deal with my problems; I only needed Him. I envisioned Him lovingly handing me the key. He told me that He had always been ready to hand it to me, but I had never asked Him to. I took the key He offered, opened the lock, and stepped into His presence. He explained everything I was struggling with, and I realized that I needed to let *Him* rule my universe.

He was by my side as we ascended the basement stairs. At the top, I let go of all my treasured boxes as I confessed and repented of my sins. Then I rededicated my life to Him. I was never the same again. I became a "new creature" in Christ. He proceeded to take the key from my hands, locking the door behind us, and then He handed the key back to me, telling me that He would never revisit my past sins or remember them ever again, but I could if I chose to. Puzzled, I asked what He meant. He told me that I could go back down there to my rooms if I chose to and sit on my throne in sin. But that by His grace, I had the Holy Spirit inside of me and He would give me the strength not to visit my basement again if I would only choose to believe and trust Him. I decided that I would let Jesus be on His throne, and I would allow my life to be ruled by Him.

Through this process I learned that sometimes God lets us fall hard, with heartbreaking injuries so that we will look up to see His face and truly be willing to learn about His love, mercy, and grace. I learned that He wants to be the ruler over my life, and for very good reasons. Although many times I find myself trying to sneak back onto my throne, my beautiful chair, as if He weren't looking, I recognize that by His grace, I have become more disciplined and content. I have found that He knows a lot more about me than I do, and His Holy Spirit will help me make the right choices when my flesh wants to do its thing. I understand now who rightly sits on the throne and who is to be glorified, and it certainly isn't me.

Sometimes, especially when I am tired, I know that Satan tempts me. Things are different in that now when I consciously start feeling that I need to go back down to the basement to languish in my messy bed of guilt or waltz to the depressing music of my past, singing words about my shattered dreams and broken promises while I dance, I remember who I am and that I have the Spirit of the Living God in me and He gives me the strength to turn away from the temptation. I am a new creature in Jesus Christ, a member of His church which is His bride. One day He will come on His white horse to rescue me from my enemies and there will be the happily ever after I've always dreamed of. The best part is that while this may sound like a fairytale, it is real!

He makes His desires my desires, allowing me to see His purposes and plans. He gives me joy while I am here on earth. Without the joy of the Lord, I would become depressed and unable to be an obedient, productive worker in His kingdom, but when I walk in spirit and truth, I am transformed by the renewing of my mind. I am able to see the world with the eyes and mind of Christ. We must do battle with our evil pride, but we must allow the Holy Spirit to work and fight through us. We cannot do it in our flesh. I have learned that when I'm faced with the temptation to sin, though my flesh is weak, I have His Holy Spirit to fight and conquer through me. We cannot fight merely in our flesh because evil is powerful. So, when we do, we are led to believe that our feelings and emotions are true when they are not. Only the word of God is real and true.

I now understand that the joy of the Lord is my strength (Nehemiah 8:10), and to count it all joy when hardship comes because through Him I *can* overcome! That realization alone is something to rejoice about. In scripture we are commanded many times to be joyful, and to rejoice eternally. Without His joy, our spirits search for something to fill the void, and we will substitute with earthly pleasures that ultimately lead to misery and separation from God. As Christians, if we succumb to being self-centered and depressed, then we will be weak and hindered in our work for Him. Our Christian walk will have its trials and tribulations. He tells us that Himself in John 16:33: "I have told you these things so that in me you may have peace. In this world you will have trouble. But take heart! I have overcome the world!"

I can still rejoice, however, because through Him, I have His Holy Spirit living in me. I rejoice because in Him, my spirit has found its place and purpose for eternity. I have finally learned to simply trust Him, especially now that I can use my past sins to help someone else. I hope that through my story you will see there can be forgiveness from your sins, too, that you don't have to keep going back to your "basement," and to help guide you to Jesus if you fall from your "throne." He alone is worthy to be praised, the Creator of the universe and beyond!

Here is a summary of things I have learned:

- He alone is God, I am not.
- I am created to bring glory and honor to God, not myself.
- I cannot know the true meaning of joy without giving myself to Jesus Christ.
- Joy and happiness are not the same. Joy does not depend on my life circumstances.
- We all have a deep yearning for fellowship with God.
- Pride is the root of all evil.
- Every morning when I awake, my flesh begins to crawl toward the throne. Therefore, I must choose every day to exalt Him, submit to Him, and to walk in spirit and in truth, or I will walk in the flesh.
- In order to maintain my joy, it is vital that I stay in continuous fellowship with Him.

- We know that God causes everything [my good *and* my bad] to work together for the good of those who love God and are called according to his purpose for them (Romans 8:28).
- The joy of the Lord is my strength to overcome my flesh and the evil that seeks to devour me.
- He forgives our darkest sins and never remembers them again.
- We can choose to be joyful or gloomy.
- Bad things happen to Christians, but He is always there to help us, to give us hope and knowledge of our glorious future with Him. Therein lies the peace that surpasses all understanding when we trust Him and that all will be well in His will. "Do not be anxious about anything, but in every situation, by prayer and petition, with thanksgiving, present your requests to God. And the peace of God, which transcends all understanding, will guard your hearts and your minds in Christ Jesus (Philippians 4:6-7).
- He uses my past to help others and me to have joy and a victorious future.
- I can do all the things that He commands me to do by the Holy Spirit when my flesh cannot.
- In Him, my spirit has finally found its place and purpose.
- I can forgive those who have hurt me, and I can love and show mercy to those who are unlovable and undeserving of mercy. I can do this because the love of the Holy Spirit is in me.
- I am a new creature in Christ Jesus.
- His mercies are new every morning! If I sin against Him, He offers me a new start with my every breath and beat of my heart.
- I cannot be forgiven unless I forgive those who sin against me. I may not ever be able to forget, but I can choose to forgive by the power of the Holy Spirit so that I, too, may be forgiven.

CHAPTER 3

Infertility Issues

On April 3, 1993, after five years of dating, I married my high school sweetheart. We set out to begin our lives together that day and only God could have orchestrated the plans He had for our family. As a little girl I had always dreamed and even talked about how many children I would have when I was all grown up, but little did I know that my plans would not line up with God's plans on that subject. I slowly began to see how much we take for granted in our everyday assumptions. Proverbs 16:9 says as much: "In their hearts humans plan their course, but the Lord establishes their steps."

Life as newlyweds was good. I was finishing college and looking forward to a career in teaching, which perfectly fit with my love for children. We knew that we wanted children of our own one day but had planned to wait until I had a teaching job before starting our family. Days turned into months and months turned into years, and so our story begins. In 2 Peter 3:8-9 it says, "But do not forget this one thing, dear friends: With the Lord a day is like a thousand years, and a thousand years are like a day. The Lord is not slow in keeping his promise, as some understand slowness . . . "

It was in the early part of our marriage that I began to be plagued by daily abdominal and back pain, not to mention the fact that the birth control pills I took were making me very sick. After months of suffering I decided to make an appointment with my OB/GYN. I described the pain and the daily struggle, but much to my dismay she did not empathize with me and seemed to downplay my symptoms. The appointment ended with her saying that if it did not improve, the only option would be for her to perform a scope procedure to see what was going on. I went home disappointed but told myself that eventually things would get better. However, months went by with no change, so I decided to stop taking birth control pills and to take other precautions while ultimately leaving the outcome up to God.

I was in the last year of college with student teaching fast approaching. To say life was busy is an understatement. The nausea went away but unfortunately the physical hurt did not. My new young husband was very understanding even though my discomfort was affecting every area of our marriage. I knew something had to change so I scheduled another appointment with my doctor. Although she still did not seem very empathetic, she scheduled me for an exploratory laparoscopy. The date was set for surgery, and we anxiously hoped for answers. Finally, the day came, and my doctor went in to investigate. The surgery revealed endometriosis and a few cysts on my ovaries. She also performed another small procedure to hopefully alleviate some of the discomfort I was experiencing during intimacy caused by the smallness of my female anatomy. Again, the pain was dismissed as a minor issue, and my doctor suggested that if I would take ibuprofen, I would be fine. At that point I began to question whether this was all just in my head as she seemed to be indicating.

The busyness of our lives continued. I was in the process of finishing up college while also working, and both my husband and I remained very involved with activities in our church. I knew as a young wife that the struggle with daily discomfort and fatigue could not be normal, but I did the best I could to press on and to engage in normal activities despite the pain. I began to wonder what was really going on with my body since I had not taken birth control pills in years but had not experienced any pregnancy scares at all. Now, after five years of marriage, a baby would be a blessing to us. My husband adored babies and children, and I always knew what a wonderful dad he would be. In fact, this is one of the things that I loved most about him. The earlier years were filled with starting a career, more school, family time, church and friends, and of course my ongoing health battle. While our lives seemed very full on the outside, we began to talk and pray. We both felt like we were at a point in our lives where we were ready to start a family. The real question was whether this would be what God wanted for us at that time.

The months and years of waiting were hard on me physically, and they took a toll emotionally as well. The back and abdominal pain that I was experiencing was continually getting worse instead of better and to add to that, it seemed that all my friends had already started or were beginning to start families. Still, God enabled us to keep a joyful heart and to show happiness for others even during our struggle. The biggest reminder of our inability to have children was always the Mother's Day recognition service at church. It was so difficult to be surrounded by mommas and babies knowing how much we wanted a baby of our own. Thoughts of *Will we ever have a baby?* flooded our minds. Knowing the heartache this caused me, my husband always remained so positive and encouraging. I kept busy by pouring my heart and soul into teaching and coaching and loving on my students and players. My husband spent a lot of time serving in the youth ministry and going on mission trips with the church to Argentina. These activities were all very rewarding, but still, they did not take the place of the child we longed for.

In October 1999, after six years of marriage we would finally begin to see some answers concerning my health issues. I'll never forget, the night before the Fall Festival at school was to take place, I was awakened by the absolute worst pain in my right side. I got out of bed and went to lay in the recliner until early morning. I finally had to wake my husband because it became so bad that I knew we had to go to the hospital. A surgeon was called in for possible appendicitis. However, he was leaning toward a possible female issue as the source of my problem, so he wanted to call my OB/GYN doctor in to get her opinion. Knowing how little she had done to help me in the past, I elected to see a new doctor in town that everyone seemed to love. The two doctors had differing opinions as to what might be going on, so they agreed that an exploratory surgery was the best answer. It turned out that it was appendicitis as was earlier suspected, but after I was settled in a room for recovery, my new OB/GYN doctor paid me a visit as well to deliver news that would begin to explain the source of some of my other difficulties. He said, "While in surgery I noticed that you have a serious case of endometriosis, which means you are going to need another surgery to remove some of that in about three months or so, after you've had time to heal from the appendectomy."

The possibility of finally being pain free and able to get pregnant was encouraging, to say the least.

One thing I was learning through this journey was never to ask someone when they were going to have a baby. I can't tell you the number of times we were asked that question. We knew people didn't have a clue about the problems we were experiencing. When people would ask us if we planned to have a child, we would just smile and say, "When God's ready for us to."

The three months passed, and it was time for the next surgery. My new doctor diagnosed me with one of the worst cases of stage four endometriosis that he had ever seen. It had attached itself to my bladder and colon and to all my female organs as well, which resulted in him having to do his best to put one of my ovaries back together. I also had a huge cyst that he removed along with the endometriosis as he worked to repair the damage that had been done to my body. Finally, someone who provided answers to all the pain and years of infertility and validated that my suffering truly was physical and not just in my mind. He was hopeful that this would resolve the issues I had been experiencing, and at the recheck appointment he was cautiously optimistic that our chances of becoming pregnant would be better.

Again, I was disappointed to find that even with the surgery and my wonderful doctor's best efforts, my suffering did not diminish. My doctor now felt that it was time for me to see a pelvic pain specialist in Birmingham, Alabama, who was not only a renowned doctor, but also the most wonderful Christian man. On my first visit with him, I left with seven different diagnoses and yet another scheduled surgery. This surgery would be major as I was diagnosed with pelvic congestion which required that he perform a procedure called a "uterine suspension." His hopes were that after the surgery my chances of becoming pregnant would increase. So, surgery number four was scheduled right away.

I was a little down and out at the seriousness of the diagnoses and dreaded facing yet another surgery, but I was also anxious to feel better. Our hopes of being able to have a baby of our own were also dwindling. I cannot say enough about how supportive and encouraging my husband remained. I remember him telling me that if we never had a baby it would be okay, and that we could always adopt. I will admit that God had begun to put little thoughts in my head concerning adoption. But I laid those thoughts aside for the time being as the surgery arrived and we again focused on hoping and praying for the best outcome. I will never forget the prayer this doctor prayed for me before surgery. He specifically prayed that God would grant him the ability to perform the surgery to the best of his ability and that God would bless us with a family one day. I had never had a doctor pray with me before, and it meant so much to me and my husband. He performed the surgery and even with that beautiful prayer, to this day I can honestly say that it was the worst surgery I've ever had. However, the doctor's belief was that after I had time to heal from surgery my pain would be so much better if I ever actually did get pregnant.

After six long weeks of recovery at home I was finally able to return to normal activities. I remember those days and the depression I battled as I wrestled with all I had been through, along with thoughts that a twenty-seven-year-old woman like myself should not be going through all of this. I remember praying but still not understanding what God was doing in our lives, and while I was never angry with God, I was heartbroken. I can't say exactly what my husband was feeling because somehow his faith never seemed to be shaken. Lamentations 3:25-26 says, "The Lord is good to those whose hope is in him, to the one who seeks him; it is good to wait quietly for the salvation of the Lord."

I continued to go for check-ups with my Christian specialist every three months, and while each time he was encouraging and optimistic, months and even years went by and still no pregnancy. My husband and I continued with our lives of teaching, coaching, and ministry, and now in addition to that, my precious dad's health began to decline rather quickly. I was a daddy's girl, and watching him suffer along with trying to process the reality of losing him only added to my emotional pain. I spent as much time as I could helping my mom care for him, staying at the hospital many times, as well as going to doctor's appointments and trying to visit each day after school. But even with all of this to occupy my mind and fill my time, with each passing day we still yearned for a baby to hold.

Time was passing and those little God whispers about adoption continued to prick my heart. We finally decided we would visit an adoption agency in Birmingham but were disappointed to find that adoption was very costly, and God just didn't give us peace about pursing it. By now we had shared with our church family about our struggle with infertility. They began to join us in praying that God would bless us with a child. Twice we heard about a baby we might adopt through friends at church. Both times I got so excited, only to be let down. Our families were also very encouraging and supportive, and I remember my sister who works at a local hospital always trying to cheer me up by saying, "We are going to get y'all a baby."

Five years had now passed since my surgery. Things were beginning to get even harder emotionally because my dad was officially diagnosed with lung cancer, and we knew that time was not on our side. In those last months and days, I tried to steal as many moments with him as I could. In February

2005 my dad lost his battle with cancer, but he gained his heavenly home. I can't describe the sadness and pain, and oddly, even the joy I felt during these days as I processed this huge loss. I was only thirty-two years old, and I was completely overwhelmed. The upcoming days were spent trying to help my mom, brother, and sisters get through this very difficult time in our lives. Our faith remained strong, but by now my husband and I didn't even talk about a baby anymore. Only an occasional mention was made by either of us about possibly looking further into adoption, as we let the days pass us by.

A little over a year after my dad passed away, May 11, 2006 started out as an ordinary day. My husband went to work, and I went to school to teach my precious second graders. I walked into my classroom after lunch and heard my cell phone ringing. I was a little startled because it was my sister calling, and I was afraid something might be wrong. I answered with a quick "Hello?" and as long as I live, I will never forget her words that came rushing back at me. She said, "There is a baby, but you've got to find a lawyer within thirty minutes."

All I could manage to say was, "*Whaaaat?*" She quickly explained that there was a baby that we could possibly adopt but we had to have a lawyer call and speak with the social worker at the hospital within thirty minutes. I remember her giving me the name and number of the social worker and then we hung up. My mind was racing, as I was thinking about how to get a lawyer. Quickly my thoughts turned to our pastor. I immediately began calling the church office, but they informed me that he was in a meeting. All sorts of emotions were flooding my mind, but I knew I needed to call my husband and tell him the news and hope that he would know of a lawyer. When he answered his phone, I hurriedly told him the same thing my sister had told me, that there was a baby, but we needed a lawyer. He was as shocked as I was, and said, "Slow down, what's going on?"

But I didn't have any more details, other than we needed a lawyer quickly. He proceeded to tell me that he had a lawyer he had used with his business. It was obvious that God was already working in ways that I could never imagine. I called his lawyer and was told that he was also in a meeting, but that they would be happy to transfer me to his partner. The secretary transferred the call, and I began to explain to this man that I had never met that there was a newborn baby at a local hospital that my husband and I could possibly adopt. I explained my worries of not being able to adopt the baby because we had not done a home study or anything to prepare for adoption. I assured him that we were good Christian people, and I tried to give him our pastor's number for a reference, but he kindly assured me that would not be necessary. I was in dismay and proceeded to give him the social worker's information. As we ended the conversation he said, "I think I know how we can get all of this worked out. I'll call you later this afternoon."

As I hung up the phone, I can't describe the feelings of excitement, fear, thankfulness, shock, and the many other emotions that are now only a blur to me. I recall my co-worker coming over in the middle of the phone conversations and taking my students to her room for me. She was also in shock at our sudden news and seemed almost as excited as I was. I then called my husband back to give him the news the lawyer had given me. I really don't think he was very confident that all of this would work out because he warned me not to get too excited just in case things fell through, which in the back of my mind, I knew was a very real possibility. And so, the waiting began.

I hung up the phone and headed to one of the tables at the back of my classroom and began to pray. I remember talking to God that day in the most intimate way, begging Him for this baby if it was His will. I recall praying and asking for this baby to love and to change my life for the better as I cried in awe of what this baby would mean to us. At that point I didn't know the sex of the baby or any other details, but we didn't care about any of that. As hard as it was to concentrate, I went back to teaching for the rest of the day. Three o'clock came and went, and still, no call.

Around 4:20, the phone began to ring and the news on the other end would change our lives forever. It was the lawyer and he began by saying, "You and your husband can go meet your new baby tonight." Those words will be etched in my mind forever. He proceeded to tell me that the baby was a five-week premature little boy weighing five pounds two ounces and measuring only sixteen inches long. He gave me a few details about the birth mom and shared that although she had some reservations about us living so close, she had agreed to the adoption. The lawyer explained that we could take our driver's licenses to the nursery at the hospital that night and meet our precious baby boy. Had God really made it that simple?? The resounding answer was YES! Yes, He had. I hung up from that call and began jumping for joy right where I was standing in the gym, thanking God for answering my prayers. What an awesome God we serve! My husband and I quickly got ready and headed to the hospital, notifying our family while we were on the way. They were in shock and disbelief just as we were because we hadn't done anything to prepare for an adoption. I cannot begin to explain the excitement and anticipation as we drove to the hospital that evening. God was doing something in our lives that could only be done by Him, and we will forever give Him all the glory, honor, and praise.

The long years, months, days, and even minutes of waiting and praying for our baby were about to come to fruition. We arrived at the nurse's desk that night nervous and excited and the sweet nurses escorted us to the nursery to meet our very own newborn baby boy. As we laid eyes on our precious baby, tears of joy and unimaginable love flooded our hearts. He was perfect, and thoughts of how anyone would be willing to give their precious baby to us was overwhelming. We got to hold and love on our baby in a storage room in the nursery that night. It was the only place they had for us to go, but it didn't matter to us where we were if we were with him. We could not quit staring at him and thanking God for this precious miracle baby. We got to spend hours with him that night and the bond of love between us was instant. It truly all seemed like an unbelievable dream. As it says in Matthew 19:26, "Jesus looked at them and said, 'With man this is impossible, but with God all things are possible.'"

The nurses were so kind to us and explained when we came back the next morning that they would give us a room where we could have visitors just as though I had given birth. We were beyond thrilled, and although we didn't want to leave him that night, we knew we had things we needed to get and people we needed to tell. Our first stop was my sister's house. God had used her in His plan to give us the desires of our heart, and we will be forever grateful to her. There was no sleep that night as thoughts flooded our minds. We continued to pray for the birth mom to sign papers the next morning, and we also began to think of the perfect name for our new baby boy. The name that God gave us was William A. and we would call him Will. My dad's name was Willie, my husband's great grandfather was Will, and his middle name was a fourth-generation name that was handed down. But most importantly, his name would be Will because he was God's will for our lives.

The next day would prove to be very exciting as well as emotional. We were able to keep Will in the room with us that day as our family, friends, and church family quickly began to bring gifts. I remember dressing Will all in blue. He was so beautiful as we held him and cuddled him. Later that afternoon the social worker came in to tell us that his birth mom had signed the adoption papers, but she wanted to see him briefly before being discharged. My mom was worried that she might change her mind if she saw him, but my response was simply, "If she does, it will be all right because he is her baby."

Thankfully for us she didn't, and we will be forever grateful for the precious gift and blessing that she gave us in Will. Our dream had come true in a matter of twenty-four hours. We were able to take Will home that day and the outpouring of love began. We had nothing for a baby but by the time we arrived home, my family, school family, church family, and our community had filled our front porch with everything we needed. I will never forget the excitement, joy, and encouragement that the whole town had for us. We could never thank everyone enough for the blessings they were to us during the most wonderful time in our lives. God had given us the most amazing miracle in our baby, but we had no idea that our story wasn't finished.

Our days with Will were so precious. We soaked up every minute with him, while continuing to thank God every day for our blessing. Every time I thought of his birth mom and her sacrifice in sharing her baby, it was unfathomable to me. We never got to meet Will's birth mom before she left the hospital that day, but I hoped that she knew the thankfulness and love I would always have for her. Our family was finally complete and the love that we had for this baby melted our hearts. We knew we would probably never have a biological child, but we did not care because it was just as if I had given birth to Will because he was ours.

A couple of months went by and it was nearly time for my regular checkup with my wonderful specialist. I was so excited because I had just gotten Will's three-month pictures, and I couldn't wait to share them with him. I knew he would be so happy for us. On the day of my appointment, I saw the nurse first and I told her that I had been having some hot flashes and that my heart had been fluttering. She wrote it all down and sent me to give my usual urine sample. I went into the room and anxiously waited to show Will's pictures to the doctor. Little did I know that the words he spoke as he entered the room that day would forever change our lives for the second time. As he swung that door open, he said, "Well, praise the Lord, you are pregnant!"

I think my heart skipped all kinds of beats that day because I couldn't believe what I was hearing. Could it really be that after thirteen years of marriage, years of pain and prayers, topped off by a miracle baby through adoption, that we were finally being blessed with our own biological child?! Tears began to flow from my eyes and my doctor said, "Don't cry, Will needs a baby brother or sister."

I was in complete shock and disbelief. My emotions were indescribable. I had great joy, but I also felt fear. I was afraid that Will would not get all the attention and love that I wanted just for him. I know those might sound like crazy emotions, but I never wanted him to feel differently because he was adopted. The nurse informed me that I needed to have an ultrasound to see how far along I was in the pregnancy. Laying on the table that day watching the flutter of my precious baby's heart beating is a sight and feeling that I will never forget. At that moment it was real, we were going to have a baby. I called my husband from the room to tell him the wonderful news, and he could not believe what he was hearing. The excitement in his voice was apparent. To be honest, I didn't know what to feel that day. I was happy, but it did take me a little while to get over the shock, especially since I was also caring for a new baby. The ultrasound showed that I was six weeks pregnant and our new precious baby would arrive in April. God was still writing our story, and I was reminded once again that only He knew the blessings that He had in store for us.

I wish I could say that the rest of my pregnancy was great, but it was hardly that at all. I was very sick at the beginning and my husband helped more than ever by taking care of Will when I wasn't able. During those nine months we doted on Will every moment, but we were eagerly awaiting the arrival of our baby girl. Yes, Will was going to have a sister!

On April 9, 2007, Will's baby sister was born. They were almost eleven months apart to the day. She came into this world weighing 7lbs. 3 oz. and measuring 21 ½ inches long. We could not have been happier! We named our new baby after a precious little girl that I had taught in second grade. She was a special ray of sunshine, and I loved her name and had even told her if I ever had a little girl, I would name her after her. Again, we were praising God and giving Him all the glory, honor, and praise for blessing us so abundantly. After all the years we spent longing for a baby, I never would have dreamed in a million years that God would bless us with two babies in a year's time. Our hearts were as full as our arms! What a journey we had been on and now our lives were complete and filled with so much joy. I can't describe the love that I had for these precious babies. The gift of Will through adoption was our first miracle from God, and then the birth of our daughter biologically was our second miraculous answer to prayer. We were tremendously blessed and living proof of Psalm 37:4, "Delight yourself in the Lord, and He will give you the desires of your heart." Only God could write this story. He has been so faithful to us during our lives and I'll never quit telling of the precious miracles He blessed us with.

One of the biggest things that God taught us in our trials was that His timing is always perfect. Sometimes in the middle of our hardships, we tend to feel our prayers and cries to God aren't being heard because we may not see immediate change in our situations. For us, it took thirteen years to see our prayers answered, but we put our trust in God's hands because "God is greater than our heart and he knows everything" (1 John 3:20). We also learned that God's timing is always perfect, even when we cannot see it. Ecclesiastes 3:1 says that "There is a time for everything, and a season for every activity under the heavens."

There are so many little and big things that God has taught me on this journey, but Proverbs 3:5-6 sums it up. "Trust in the Lord with all your heart and lean not on your own understanding; in all your ways submit to him, and he will make your paths straight." As I look back and reflect, I am very thankful for the trials that we faced because God helped us grow in so many ways just as He continues to grow us today. My prayer for Will and our daughter is that they will always know how very special they are and that they remember that they are true miracles from God, loved by God, and loved by us more than words could ever tell. We absolutely love the story that God has written for us. Just know that whatever you may be facing, God has already written your story, too.

CHAPTER 4

Infidelity and Abortion

"For you created my inmost being; you knit me together in my mother's womb. I will praise you because I am fearfully and wonderfully made; your works are wonderful, I know that full well. My frame was not hidden from you when I was made in the secret place, when I was woven together in the depths of the earth. Your eyes saw my unformed body; all the days ordained for me were written in your book before one of them came to be." Psalm 139:13-18

Abortion is recognized by some as the most "unthinkable act" done by any female and as something that is unnatural for any mother. It is sometimes too hard for me to acknowledge that I did something that I have never believed in. I was told that my baby was just a "blob of tissue" and I made myself believe the lie so that I could justify my actions. Yes, I am one of the four in ten women that you might be sitting next to in church that has had an abortion.

Before I get into the actual story of my abortion, I feel the need to share a little about myself and my life growing up. My father died when I was three years old so there was never a male figure in my life that I really looked up to in filling that role. My mom dated one person for a considerable length of time, and he was probably the closest thing I had to a father figure. However, they broke up and he, too, was out of my life. She did eventually remarry, but to a very abusive man, so I still did not know what a loving father was supposed to look like. I'm sure I attempted to find aspects of that missing role model in my life through other relationships, but I was never able to fill that void.

As a young child I went to church with my grandmother. After she passed away during my teenage years, I found a church that had a great youth group and started going there. My mother and stepfather did not attend, but my grandmother always made sure that I did. I accepted Christ when I was around thirteen years old. I'm not sure that I really knew the full meaning of what I had done at that point in my life, but I felt like I had finally found the Father I was missing, the One I would love and Who would love me like His child in return. In the coming years I would turn my back and disappoint Him repeatedly, but I found that He still never turned His back on me.

Fast forward a few years to when I was eighteen and newly graduated from high school. I met the man that soon became my husband. I remember telling my mother, "This is the one."

I really hadn't had too many boyfriends before then, and I fell for this man like no other. I got pregnant and because I didn't want to have a baby out of wedlock, we got married. There was never any talk about abortion or adoption. We had dated for about seven months, and we just jumped right into marriage even though we didn't really know each other like we should have.

Obviously, at this point I was no longer following God's direction but had put Him on a shelf and tucked Him neatly away while I did whatever I wanted to do in my life. I was nineteen years old, my husband was twenty, and we had a new baby boy to care for. Around this time, we moved away from my family and friends so that my husband could pursue his career in the entertainment business.

As an entertainer, my husband had "groupies," as they were called in the music industry. These were usually young girls who would follow the entertainer to wherever he was performing. I remember the first affair, but there would be many more. Unfortunately, infidelity became part of our marriage from the very beginning. Every time I would find out about an affair he had, the confrontation would start out with his complete denial followed by a huge fight that ended with him saying he was sorry, and that he would never do it again. I would forgive him and then nothing would be said about it until the next argument when I would drag it back up and throw it in his face. Looking back now, I don't know how I kept up the facade of a perfect marriage. I told no one what life was really like because I didn't want to tarnish our appearance as the happy little family—which was the farthest thing from what we were. But we were both good at pretending, even while we were hurting on the inside. We couldn't keep up the front forever, though, and we eventually did separate a couple of times. I regret to say that during those times I, too, saw other people.

When my son was about five years old, there was a sweet lady that lived across the street from us who asked if she could take my son to church with her. I agreed, and every Sunday she would pick him up and make sure he was there. God was throwing me lifesavers over and over, but I ignored them. Then one morning I thought to myself, *What am I doing? I should be taking my own child to church.* I remember I was watching a church program on television and a famous singer-songwriter, B. J. Thomas, shared his testimony and it made a big impact on me. I fell to my knees right there in my living room and for the second time I surrendered my life to the Lord. I knew this encounter was nothing like what I experienced as a teenager, though. God was real to me now, and I began then to learn about His love for me. I started to follow His Word and to develop the relationship with Him that I had wanted for so long. After the terrible loneliness I felt in my marriage, I had finally found the one thing that filled the void. Time after time, I tried to get my husband to come to church with us, but he would have nothing to do with it. I shared my testimony at my new church, thinking that he would at least come to support me in that, but he refused, saying that he wasn't ready. We went on with our pretentious marriage, acting for everyone else's benefit as if everything was perfect. I was in church now with my son, and I was finding peace in my life, even though my husband's affairs continued.

We had two more children over the next five years. I was now in my thirties, and at the encouragement of a good friend, I entered college. I decided to start taking some classes, with the mindset that I would figure out along the way what I really wanted to do. Little did I know at the time that this path was a God thing in my life. I was following His lead into these unknown territories and trying to have faith in where He led me. I was like the Israelites wandering through the desert to the promised land: grumbling, lacking faith, and at times losing sight of the big picture. But despite that, I made it through college while raising three children and finally obtained my bachelor's degree in Nursing. I was very proud of this accomplishment. It gave me a new level of confidence knowing that I could now contribute and help my family financially.

I had worked nights for about two years when once again I knew that something was "off" in our marriage. I didn't want to go down that path, but a woman's intuition kicks in, and everything in me knew that my husband was having another affair.

It was during this time that I got pregnant again with our fourth child. My husband said that we couldn't afford another child because we were barely making ends meet as it was, bringing in just enough money for us to survive. Never in my wildest dreams would I have ever expected to hear the words that would come out of his mouth next. He said, "You need to get an abortion."

He told me to talk to my doctor, who was a good friend of ours. This doctor also agreed that an abortion might be a good choice since it hadn't been too long since I had given birth to my last child. Why did I listen to this, and why did I even let them talk me into considering abortion as an option? Satan made his way into the picture just like he had done so many times before. I believed the lie that my tiny baby was just a "blob of tissue."

I didn't have any intervening circumstances or anyone to sway me away from this decision. I didn't see any flashing signs from God telling me, "No, don't do this!"—or maybe I just wasn't looking for them. There was not a pregnancy center available in our area that I could have gone to for support or education on fetal development. The abortion procedure was arranged by my husband. We couldn't afford to have the baby and raise it, but we did find the money to have an abortion. We simply drove up to the clinic, filled out papers, and it was done; nothing to it. Little did I know that this decision would haunt me for the rest of my life.

I was told that the procedure wouldn't take long, but it was more than just a moment. It was a moment that changed my life forever from that point forward. I remember laying on the table in that cold room with the doctors and nurses all seeming so matter of fact about what was taking place. They all seemed so cold and indifferent, like this was just an everyday thing to them. They offered no other options and tears began to run down my face. I knew how wrong this was, and I cried out to God to please forgive me. I could have stopped them at any time, but I didn't. I remember thinking to myself, *Somebody, please stop this!* and then I heard the suction turn on. My husband later told me that he had come so close to coming in the room and stopping it. I wish to God that he had.

I became a different person for the next thirty years, something that was directly related to what I had done. I was never able to openly grieve or mourn the loss of my baby. Even though I had asked God to forgive me for my sin, I couldn't open my mind to believe the extent of God's mercy and grace. He was willing to forgive me, but I had to learn to forgive myself, and let go of the guilt so that I could receive the mercy and grace that He was waiting to pour out on me. Forgiving myself was the hardest part. Through the years, I stuffed that part of my life so far down inside that I thought it would never come up again, but how wrong I was!

The crazy thing about me having this abortion is that I knew the Bible included murder as one of the "Thou shalt nots . . ." in the Ten Commandments. But regardless, I had murdered my own baby.

I was at the lowest of lows. My husband and I were fighting all the time, and my marriage was slowly deteriorating. We never discussed the abortion as we pretended it never happened. Looking back, I suffered from depression that I could not escape on my own. I was not present in my marriage, and I simply went through the motions of everyday life and took care of my children. At this point my husband was having yet another affair and seeing someone else. I knew it with all my heart and had evidence to prove it. We finally decided to separate, and he moved out. I had completely pushed God out of my life. It was like I was hiding from Him, not wanting Him to see all of this ugly mess. But I knew that He was there through it all. I believed there was no way He could still love me after all I had done. At least that is what Satan was telling me, and with all that weighing me down, he had a pretty strong hold on me. A male friend of ours came to me and confirmed what I thought to be true about my husband seeing someone and that the relationship had been going on for quite some time. I wasn't surprised. I was vulnerable and lonely at this point in my life and this friend was also happy to give me the attention I thought I so desperately needed. We ended up having an affair and as a result, I became pregnant. I was planning a trip to Alaska to see my brother and sister, so I told them my dilemma, and they helped to arrange a second abortion for me while I was there. I told myself that I had already had one abortion so a second one couldn't make God love me any less than He already did. I was scared and couldn't tell my soon to be ex-husband that I was pregnant with someone else's child. As crazy as it sounds, I was still hoping that our marriage might possibly survive. I thought I could just get rid of this "problem" and then we would get back together and work things out. I felt certain I would never escape from this deep pit that seemed to be spiraling out of control.

After sharing about the excruciating emotional pain I went through with my first abortion, it is hard for me to even admit that I had a second one. Why would I choose to do this again? But what I have learned about being in the depths of depression is that your mind just doesn't process things the same as it normally would.

I remember going through the last abortion experience as if it was nothing. I never acknowledged it. But even years later when the word abortion would come up among my friends or in the news, I would cringe and lower my head as tears would flood my eyes. To be totally honest, I was still trying unsuccessfully to find complete healing from the second one. I prayed over and over to God begging Him to forgive me, even though He forgave me the *first* time I ever asked. I have not shared this part of my life with very many people because even though I know I'm forgiven, I have struggled with understanding the experience myself.

Afterwards, many times, I felt hopeless. At one point I even thought, *If things stay this way, I don't know if I can go on.* Looking back, these experiences taught me that God was with me through every detail, even when I didn't see Him or feel Him. And that's how I survived. I see His plans more clearly today than yesterday. Turning the page is difficult, but I now have a peace about my life, my choices, and His love for me that can only come from God.

Fast forward with me several years to a Sunday morning when I was in church and a speaker from a local pregnancy center came to talk about their wonderful organization. With permission, she shared that another one of our church members had recently come forward about her own abortion. Just hearing that someone like me that went to church every Sunday and had a relationship with our Lord could come forward and admit to the whole congregation this secret she had held in for years was the open invitation I needed to come forward, too, and find the healing I so desperately sought. I made a point to meet the speaker, and I even scheduled a time to stop by the office to learn more about her ministry. Little did I know that she saw right through me and had a post-abortive volunteer prepared to meet me on the day I visited her office.

What I learned from this sweet soul was that God loved me, and He loved me through all those dark days I had walked through. It was finally time for me to see a glimpse of His light shining on me. The healing from this choice isn't a one-time thing where you snap your fingers and everything in your heart is fine. No, it's been a process, and I'm still learning to love myself daily. It's different now when I get a little down in my emotions or hear the word abortion. I am free from that deep gut-wrenching pain I once felt. Now it's replaced by a love and peace that only God can provide.

God cared all along, and He had a plan for me that was much better than I could ever have imagined. I remarried to a wonderful man that loves me and my children like they are his own. Due to my emotional baggage, I tried my best to sabotage the relationship, but he stuck with me through thick and thin. We have now been married twenty years. I shared my story with him and with my children, which is something that I thought I could never do, and they all accepted my story with grace. As they realized that they would have had another brother or sister, they all had different responses. They still don't know about the second abortion. I'm believing that God has a plan for the day when it's time for them to know, and I'm patiently waiting to see how that will unfold. Not to say that I'm not a little scared, but I feel that part of my confession is another step in my healing and one that I still must walk through.

I now volunteer at a local pregnancy center like the one that came to my church. I share my story with other girls and women who are in situations that are similar to mine. Hopefully, my story will help to enlighten others about what abortion does to a person physically, emotionally, and spiritually. Mostly, I hope my story will help them to see the love Christ has for them and that they can depend on Him to get them through any situation if they will only have faith to believe.

I tell you my story, but I want to stress that what I have done in my past doesn't define who I am today. Even with all my failures, I know that God loves me and has completely forgiven me. Those feelings of guilt and shame I once felt so strongly as I listened to Satan's lies have continually faded through the years of healing. I want you to hear that if you have been down this same road, He still loves you and is willing to forgive you, too. Just ask Him, and then walk with Him through the healing journey. Sometimes Satan still attempts a jab from time to time, but I quickly come back with "NOT TODAY SATAN!" and I hope that you will, too.

CHAPTER 5

Secret Struggles: A Birthmother's Perspective

How in the Sam Hill, as my daddy would say, did my senior year spin so out of control? As a seventeen-year-old, I had already joined the workforce (well, part-time anyway) through a program at school that prepared students to work a job and earn money while completing their final classes before graduation. I was the tall and slender brunette, a middle-class girl raised by Christian parents who loved me and my younger sister and taught us that there was only one way to live, which was "by the Good Book."

I was a daddy's girl, sticking close to his side all through my childhood. He was always happy to involve me in whatever he was doing, instructing and educating me just as a teacher would explain a project for a student. He had common sense and used it in anything he did, from repairs at home to teaching a Bible class at church. I loved him so much and believed that he could do no wrong. He expected me to try anything, because in his words, "You can do anything you set your mind to." Dad was an electrician by trade, and he loved shortwave radios. He built several of his own Ham radios for the purpose of being a part of a network of radio operators that helped people in emergency situations, such as when tornadoes struck. I had almost mastered Morse code by the age of fourteen, until I began to be distracted by the idea of handsome teenage boys.

I was also infatuated with hot cars at this age, those muscle cars with rumbling engines. I wanted one for myself, and I set out to get one. I kept my eyes on the local car lots for weeks and spotted one that I really liked. It was a 1956 Chevy with a "bad" sounding small block engine. A four-in-the-floor (4 speed shifter) and wide tires; exactly what I was after. I enjoyed the attention that the car brought me, and I learned—from my dad of course—how to change tires, how to check my oil and transmission fluid, and how to replace sparkplugs and wires to keep it running smoothly. I had quite a few conversations with young men about that car, which was enough to pique interest in this high school girl that drove such a cool ride.

My part-time job gave me an open window to interact with customers and people I might not otherwise have met. There was one young man that I would check out at my register that had noticed me driving to and from work in the afternoons after school. He was giving me those long looks, and a wink which flattered the "dickens" out of me. One afternoon he asked what time I got off work and if he could talk to me a little while after, maybe buy me a coke. I told him I was okay with that, although he was several years older than me. I found out later that he was eight years older than me to be exact, and that he had been in the military and even served a tour in Vietnam. These red flags should have stopped me in my tracks. After all, I knew that this man would not pass the approval of my conservative parents. But he was fun to flirt and joke with, he was sexy, and something deep within me began to stir. My parents would never have to know. I just wouldn't tell them.

So there. I had a secret that was smokin' hot. Did I know better? Yes. But I was quite smitten by this handsome man and drawn in by this passion that felt so good. He was always fun, and in a great mood every time we were together, although it did become clear to me that his good mood was helped along by a little beer or whatever drink might be available for the evening. Another red flag. But he carried some shrapnel in him, fragments of an exploded shell in 'Nam. I excused the drinking, deciding that it helped him cope. I had been taught better than to get involved with someone with these habits, but I had allowed myself to get too deep into the emotions of this relationship. It became a little harder to hide the meetings that we discreetly arranged.

Three months turned into four, and I realized that my monthly period was late. "No," I thought, "I can't be pregnant." But I was. I'd known this *could* happen, but now it had become a reality. *How could I have been so stupid?* I can still remember the panic I felt and was trying so hard to hide, and because I had kept this relationship a secret, I had no girlfriends or anyone to confide in. I had no idea what I was going to do. It was more than I could process in my seventeen-year-old brain during the next couple of months. I knew that my parents would be devastated.

I put off telling anyone as long as I could, waiting until I was beginning to show and no longer had a choice. You can imagine how crushed my mom and dad were after I sat at the kitchen table and told them I was pregnant. They couldn't even look me in the eye. Tears flowed from all three of us, and by the end my emotions were spent. That was the lowest point of my life. Thankfully my little sister was in school and my parents managed to keep my secret from her until I was sent away to have my baby. It was the seventies, and at that time parents made the decisions for young girls in these situations. I had made enough disappointing decisions, and I was not going to question or rebel against whatever they said was best for me and my baby. My mother told me that there were couples that could not have children of their own and that they would love to adopt my baby and raise it as their own.

I had about four months to live out the rest of my pregnancy in an unwed mother's home. I became very close to the girl that took me from the entry point when I arrived to show me to my room. We bonded immediately as friends, and to this very day I consider her to be my best friend in the whole world. We were treated very kindly, but we were all expected to do certain chores in the dormitory style home that was provided. We grew up while we were there, and we felt blessed to have each other to confide in. We mostly talked about the way things were at our respective homes. My friend went into labor and gave birth to a baby boy a month before I was to give birth to my child, which, as it turned out, was also a boy. She went home after that, and my last four weeks there were so lonely without her company. We had both renewed our love for the Lord and had attended chapel together each week. The Lord got us through this low point in our lives, and I prayed that whoever was to adopt my son would give him a happy home. I was able to spend three days with my sweet baby feeding him, dressing him, and just holding him before my case worker told me that it was time for him to leave. I was numb for several days just thinking about what I'd been through, and now it was over. How was I supposed to push these emotions away, and just go back to normal life again?

I wish I could say that my emotional problems were instantly resolved, but my life was a little unsettled for the next five years after giving birth. I had managed to keep this whole thing a secret, explaining my leave from the area as a time during which I was taking special courses to prepare me for my life after high school. I had lost touch with the father of my son during my temporary exile. He had his own problems to deal with and my parents never knew the kind of situation that led up to my fall from innocence.

After several years passed, I began to feel the presence of the Lord pulling at my heart to return to my roots. I began going back to church on a regular basis, even being committed enough to attend Sunday school. God's word tells us in Matthew 18:12 that when one of the sheep wanders from the flock, the Good Shepherd will lay down His life for that one lost sheep. Praise be to Jesus for His mercy and grace! I was wandering. Getting back in church and being obedient to God's word was the turning point in my life.

A mutual friend introduced me to the man who would become my husband, and two years later we had a son who filled that big empty spot that I had known for so many years. I took great pleasure in being a mom to him, but so many memories of my firstborn came flooding back. My first child was never far from my thoughts, although the Lord had me busy raising my second baby boy. I have been so blessed over the years with family, both my own and my husband's. On many occasions as new babies were born into our circle of nieces, nephews, and cousins, my mind would drift back to thoughts of my firstborn son. The heartache was still very real. I had received a letter three months after his birth stating that he had been adopted, but that was the only information I had. Was he in this state? Were there other children in the home? Were they loving people? I prayed so much about him.

Thirty-four years went by. One Saturday I went to my hairdresser to get a haircut. My husband was home. My younger son was now grown and in military training. He had followed in his dad's footsteps by volunteering to serve in the National Guard. I came home from my hair appointment and found a name and phone number written on the note pad that I always kept near our kitchen phone. THAT NAME . . . *THAT NAME!* I recognized it as the name I had given to my firstborn. It was the name that was on his birth records. I screamed my husband's name as though the kitchen was on fire. He was in the garage tidying up, and he came running. "What?" he questioned.

I answered, "Tell me about this phone call!" I had picked up the note pad and was holding it like it was the most important paper in my life. It *was* the most important paper at that moment. "Oh, yeah," he said, "that was an unusual call. A young man, asking questions about your maiden name. I confirmed that you had that name. Then he asked how long we had been married, and if he could speak with you. I told him you would be home in about an hour and he left his phone number and said, 'Could you have her call me? And ask her if this name means anything to her.'"

I almost came completely unglued! I had told my story to my husband before we were married, and he replied that he wasn't sure how he felt about it. I told him that it was part of my history, and I wanted him to know the truth before we were married since we might one day face the very situation that we were dealing with right now. I paced the floor and tears began to flow. But wait . . . suddenly, the pressure was on *me*. My tears stopped, because those thoughts were now racing through my brain. I had to return that call, and you better believe I *was* going to return that call no matter what. But what if he was mad? What if he was upset with this woman who would not keep him? It took me an hour and a half to get up the nerve to make the call, but I did it even though my heart was still beating twice its normal rate.

The phone was ringing. "Hello?" he said.

I replied, "This is _____. I used to be _____," and I said my maiden name.

The humble voice on the line asked, "Did you put a baby up for adoption in 1972?"

Tears began to flow non-stop. "Yes," I said with a trembling voice.

"Well, I'm him," he responded. I was crying so hard that I was sort of gasping for air.

"I'm sorry," I blubbered out. "I have been waiting on this phone call for years!"

"It's okay," he said, "go ahead. I'm in no hurry."

When I regained the ability to speak, I said, "I have two questions to ask you: Are you happy, and do you know the Lord?" A short pause and then he said, "Yes on both questions. I'm about as happy as a man can be. I have a wife and three kids. I'm very happy."

"Oh! I am a grandmother," I said.

With a little chuckle he replied, "Yes, you are. And to answer your second question, I stayed after Sunday school one Sunday to talk with our teacher, and to ask him about a few questions that I had. I prayed to receive Christ that day."

He began telling me that his beautiful wife had encouraged him to find his birth mom. After he agreed she began the process of searching records and high school rosters in the area where my address was located—my address that was listed on the birth record. There were lots and lots of phone calls and lots of dead ends. I asked him what he did for a living. "I am a police officer in the local community where I live."

And then I blurted out, "A cop. I hope you are a good cop." After those hurtful words began to sink in, I apologized for saying that to him.

"That's okay," he said. "There are bad ones, I suppose. Yes, I try to be good." He continued, "Not long ago I thought, 'If she (meaning me), still lives in our state she will have a driver's license with her picture on it.' So, I put your name in the data base in my police car, and there were two ladies that popped up with your maiden name. I called my wife out to the car and showed her what I found. The first one I pulled up didn't seem to stir a response from her. Then, I showed her the second one, and her eyes lit up. She said 'Oh my gosh! She looks just like you!'"

Well, it was my license, and from that starting point, he was able to find a current address. I was so glad that the photo on my license was a decent one, for a change!

I'm sure that you are wondering if my son also tried to find his biological father. He did ask me who his father was, and I explained to him the basic facts about our relationship and how everything came about. I had only talked to his father one time over the past thirty-something years. I contacted him about a year and a half after giving birth and told him that I had something that he might want to know about, proceeding to tell him that I had gotten pregnant and had given birth to our son whom I had placed for adoption. I told him that I knew he would not be happy about a child since he already had a child by an earlier marriage that had failed. I also told him that I didn't expect him to marry me and that I realized that we were in lust and not truly in love. The hardest part of the conversation was when I asked him if he would want to know if our son ever decided to contact me, and if he would admit that he was his father. He said yes, and that was how we left things between us.

Now, after all these years, I looked up a number based on where he used to live and found that he still lived there. I called him one day after work and told him that our son had found me and what a nice young man he was. I told him about his family and his job in law enforcement and how proud he would be of the man that our son had become. I have never heard that much silence in a phone call, ever! As it turned out, he never really thought that this would happen. He never thought that our son would call. He now had a wife and she knew nothing of this situation. I told him that I was sorry for the difficult position that he was in, but I reminded him of his promise to me years ago to admit that he was our child's father. He finally agreed to talk to him but said that he needed some time. It took him a full year to get up enough nerve to meet our son and his wife. Since then, they have also developed a good relationship between their families, and they are another set of grandparents for our grandchildren.

I cannot begin to tell you what a beautiful relationship that we have now. His wife, a registered nurse, was so kind, loving, and accepting of this nervous lady that was her mother-in-law. After our first face-to-face meeting in a Cracker Barrel that was at the half-way point between our homes, I was a little unsure about how much they would want me to be involved in their lives. But soon after our visit, my son and his wife mailed me the most beautiful grandparents' card, which was their way of letting me and my husband know that they did indeed want me to be a grandparent, and a part of their family. That moment was such a huge sigh of relief for me! I thanked God for answering prayers. The weight of years of guilt and heartache was being lifted. I cannot begin to tell you the conversations that I have had with the Lord since then. Words of thankfulness and gratitude have come from my lips because I know that this whole story was written by my God. Forgiveness has been freely given to me, and I cannot stop smiling!

About two months after our first meeting face to face, I got to meet the loving couple that adopted my son and raised him to adulthood. My family was invited to their home for a meal. They were so gracious and kind. As they showed me around their home and I saw the bedroom that had been my son's while growing up, I could imagine the love and conversation that was a part of everyday life. They had adopted a little girl after my son, so he grew up with a sister to interact with and share Christmases and other holidays.

It seems to me that the Lord has allowed me to be a part of the fabric of my son's adult life for a reason. A year after I met him his adoptive mother passed away from cancer, and within another year he lost his sister from a rare condition that no one expected would take her life. His adoptive dad is doing well to this day. We stay in touch with him, and every year I send him a Father's Day card expressing how much he means to me. He and his wife were chosen by God to raise my son and his sister, and I could tell they were great parents.

I feel like I have been blessed with this journey in part so that I can share what I've learned with others. As a result of my experience, I began volunteering with a crisis pregnancy center in our area. Although I work a full-time job, I take one day a week to volunteer at the center so that I can share hope through Christ with young girls who find themselves facing an unplanned pregnancy just as I once did. I am trained to listen to the heart and the needs of our clients and to educate them about their available options if they feel that they are not ready to parent. I share about the responsibilities that are a part of parenting, and I also educate them on abortion from a factual as well as a Christian faith perspective in hopes that they will understand the gift of life that they've been given. The other option I share is adoption, which I speak about through my personal experience regarding the emotional impact, but also the way Christ can work through that to make it a beautiful experience as well. I have found great satisfaction in sharing my story as well as the hope that Christ offers since I am so aware that He is the One that made something beautiful from the mess that I got myself into all those years ago. If He could do it for me, I know that He will do it for our girls—and you, too! The Lord continues to shape my life, and I pray that I can be His hands and feet on this earth as I encounter new friends and enjoy family—*all* my family—to the fullest.

**It should be noted that the adoption arrangement experienced by the author of this chapter is classified as a "closed adoption" arrangement and is no longer encouraged as a healthy method of placement for mothers or their babies. In today's society the most utilized form of adoption is a semi-open arrangement.

CHAPTER 6

Marriage, Ministry and Porn

NOTE: *My husband has read every word of this chapter and allowed me to share this part of his story.*

"Whatever you do, please don't open your messages when you get home." My husband's voice held panic.

"What are you talking about? What do you mean my messages?" I asked.

He replied, "Just please trust me, please do this for me, please don't look at your messages until I get home."

"I won't look, but you are freaking me out right now," I said, unsure of what I was headed into. We hung up the phone and as we said our goodbyes, I tried to hide my uneasiness. I continued home with our children. It had started as a normal day, normal schedule, and normal school pickups. But the ending to this day would prove to be anything but normal.

My husband and I met while I was a student in college. He was my campus minister. We were seventeen years apart in age, which was slightly taboo at that time from the beginning. I had no idea how old he was at first, but I loved him, and he loved me. I never doubted our ability to handle anything life might throw our way. I was young, naïve, and totally in love. However, there was nothing that could have prepared me for the journey upon which I was about to embark.

After graduating high school, my husband worked as a pipe fitter's apprentice in welding until he felt the call to ministry. He later married his first wife, had two children with her, and appeared to have a normal life as he went about ministering to others. After ten years of marriage his first wife died, leaving him with a six-year-old and a two-year-old to raise alone.

We started dating a year later. He confessed during our engagement that he had struggled with pornography ever since he had been introduced to it at age twelve. His first wife never knew, but he wanted complete honesty in our relationship. I believed he truly wanted freedom and thought that I could help him find it. I don't think either one of us realized the effects of pornography. I really didn't think it was a big deal because I thought, *Everyone has at least looked at porn at some point in their lives, right? My husband looked and acted normal. How beautiful of him to confess and want to start fresh.* I loved that he had confessed to me.

I would describe myself as an introvert, but I still like interaction with a few close friends. I am athletic, playing ball from the time I was about seven or eight years old and continuing through college. I am competitive by nature, and even as an adult I'm still slightly competitive in many things. This may have caused my husband and me to have an unhealthy fuss every now and then, but for the most part, being competitive with drive and determination I thought was a good thing. However, when you combine a competitive nature with an addict, it becomes a set up for disaster. I may have been the second wife, but there was no way I was going to be second at anything else in my marriage, so I did everything I could do to keep my husband happy. The world tells us that we must be *all* the things and that sex looks like so many different things. I had to live up to all of it.

Regardless of what I did, how often I did it, or even how we did it, he was never satisfied. One of the classic struggles that comes with pornography is that it leaves you unsatisfied in real relationships. It also creates an indescribable emptiness—emptiness not only for my husband, but an emptiness that I, too, felt but didn't understand. When it came to sex, I was an object that brought him sexual pleasure rather than a person with whom he found pleasure in sharing intimacy. The emptiness consumed him, causing him to crave more, and sex was all that seemed to matter. I was never enough, and the emptiness consumed me as well as my preferences, emotions, and other needs were left unmet.

Alcohol was a way to cope with the emptiness. The issue isn't whether a drink itself is right or wrong, but in this case the greater concern to me is the heart and the purpose I had for drinking. I drank to cope and to numb the emptiness that existed in my soul. I drank to meet demands as I continued to think I was the one that wasn't good enough. I knew I couldn't keep going like this. Just two months before the phone call I mentioned in the beginning, while my husband was out of town one night, I prayed and even wrote an entry in my journal asking God to help me be enough. "I feel like a whore," I wrote. "I can't do this anymore, God. It isn't healthy. God help me."

I asked Him to help me be a better wife, to help me meet the needs of my husband. I forgot about that journal entry and wouldn't recall it until six months later when I saw my prayers being answered in ways I never imagined.

That phone call shattered my world. I didn't know the extent of what we were battling. I didn't know what I felt or even how to simply breathe. I had given myself completely, sacrificially, and it wasn't enough. As I said before, I'm so competitive. In all that I do, I fight, I win, and I give it my heart and soul. I had exposed the core of who I really was, and I had been rejected by the one person I trusted the most. My husband was supposed to care for this heart of mine and protect it at all costs. Instead, he had sacrificed my heart and soul for a brief, selfish high and then added to that insult sexual conversations and interactions with a variety of different women and a variety of different images. Surely though, this could be fixed. After all, they were just photos, videos, and words. This had to be fixable. I don't give up. I don't quit. I don't lose.

The first step I took was to battle with my own problems. The messages my husband was referring to in the beginning of this story were messages from a woman that he was supposed to meet. Only now she was making his sin public, sending the messages not only to me, but also utilizing social media to send them to a few of our friends and contacts as well. In fear and shock, our initial reaction to being outed was to cover his tracks by touting the lie that our social media account had been hacked. We only had to lie to a select few. Our story was believable, or at least no one questioned it based on our reputation of service in the community and our image as one big happy family. From that dishonest starting point, we began quietly to battle our demons.

As I lay in bed that first night, I knew honesty was needed. The Lord convicts His people of sin, even in the hearts of those who have experienced tragedy. So, the next morning, I made a phone call to our pastor and his wife who had been close friends of ours for years. I didn't know what to tell him other than the honest, painful truth—no lies or cover ups. I knew that this was not the type of thing to be battled alone. After telling our pastor, he struggled for words. My heart was shattered on so many different levels and for so many different reasons. I needed the comfort that I knew their friendship and support would bring.

Religious circles would like to tell us that ministers don't struggle with these things. They will shout that minister's wives are supportive help mates that stand alongside their spouses and don't mention these battles because there is a ministry to protect. Our role as ministers' wives is to encourage and support our husbands at all costs. The lies scream that protection of ministry involves silence. The lies also say that wives in general are supposed to keep their husbands happy so that pornography isn't needed. Or, based on the ones shouting and the agenda they are pursuing, more worldly circles might shout that pornography encourages a more "freeing" sexual experience. With these thoughts running through my mind, especially as a minister's wife, *failure* would probably be the word that dominated my brain the most.

As we tried to fix the issues, the word *failure* became even more prominent. We counseled with our pastor, with a licensed counselor in town, and with a licensed counselor an hour away. We read multiple books, purchased protective online software, and even took advantage of medication that was supposed to help. And yet, there was little improvement. It became apparent that we were dealing with an addiction. As with every addict, if you take away the drug withdrawals will follow, and the withdrawals were not easy. As I packed a small survival bag to hide under my eighteen-month-old's crib in case the situation escalated, I again felt like a failure. We were doing everything we knew to do, and it still wasn't enough. I was so angry. I was also spiritually hurt and presently working my way through the acknowledgement that I was caught in a manipulative, emotionally, verbally, and sexually abusive marriage. I was in the process of realizing my "normal" was anything but normal. I didn't want to read my Bible, and I didn't want to pray. Everything about my life felt cold. I had given everything I had, and I had nothing left to offer. I couldn't pep talk myself out of this one. I tried to educate myself on my husband's issues, and in all of my reading and research, I didn't find one book where there was a recovery of a relationship of someone who had struggled with online affairs, pornography, sexual abuse, emotional abuse, and the deeper issue of addiction. Everything I read was recovering from one, maybe two issues, but not all of them. I learned that people don't typically go back to their abusers but recover in a new relationship as they deal with the baggage from the previous one. The only thing I could cling to was I needed the "faith of a mustard seed" (Matt 17:20).

This faith of a mustard seed brought two incredible gifts. The first was the comfort that my emotions were okay. I was reminded of Mary in the Bible. Mary, the sister of Lazarus. Mary, who wiped the feet of Jesus with her hair. Mary, who chose to sit at the feet of Jesus and was praised. Mary, who was devoted to her Lord. Mary however, unlike her sister, was not found running out to meet Jesus after Lazarus died in hopes of Him comforting her broken soul. Mary stayed back at the house. In my mind, I believe the hurt was too much. She knew Jesus could have saved her brother but instead He chose not to. The question for her had nothing to do with lack of belief. Her question was more along the lines of "Where were You?" and "Why? If You had only been here, he would not have died." I love though that Jesus calls for her. He didn't leave her in her grief alone. He calls, He comforts, He weeps, and then He performs a miracle. He comforted me, too, in my distance and heartache in other ways and through other people, but to be completely honest, there were a few weeks I couldn't pick up my Bible, and I couldn't pray. I felt His presence, but I just couldn't talk. Was it the best choice? Probably not, but it's where my heart was at the time, and I fully believe Jesus meets us where we are, then lovingly calls for us, grieves with us, and works in such a way that we see Him in a powerful new light.

The second gift the Lord gave to me was the outlet of photography. My own life was a mess. But if I could capture something beautiful and freeze it for a moment in time, whether that be real smiles of a family or the beauty found in a landscape, my heart would feel a sense of peace. The Lord gave me the ability to appreciate and see beauty in and through His creation. He comforted my soul for this journey He was allowing me to walk through. He gave strength from the few that knew. I am such a private person, but He placed in my life exactly who needed to be there to help share the burden. To those few people I will be forever grateful. The Lord is true to His promises and gives what will help us and what we need to be strong. "So do not fear, for I am with you; do not be dismayed, for I am your God. I will strengthen you and help you; I will uphold you with my righteous right hand" (Isaiah 41:10).

The comfort He gave also brought the strength to process the details I discovered. Processing is not easy, but it's important to feel the pain and work through it to heal. Shoving it down gets you nowhere. I verbalized in words to a few close friends. I photographed beautiful things. I prayed for miracles that never came in the way I wanted. More lies, more heartache, more abuse.

The children and I packed our bags and moved in with my parents for part of the summer, but with some carefully worded explanations, no one really questioned us. My husband went to Texas for a long, intensive weekend program followed by conference calls for accountability, and weekly "Sex Addicts Anonymous" meetings in another city. I graduated nursing school and secured a job right away as a nurse in postpartum and women's health care at the local hospital. I could have left him then, but following the separation, counseling in Texas, the year of marriage counseling we did in our hometown, and a whole lot of prayer, life finally began to improve.

He was better. I knew he was better, and it was so refreshing. Those two years following nursing school graduation were such a blessing. We had been through a living hell and survived only by the grace of God. My husband was sweet, tender, caring, compassionate, ministering, and I was so proud of him and all that he had battled and overcome. I loved being with him again, and our family was together again. Looking back, I know those good moments were just as real as the bad ones we had experienced. I had a God-given peace that I couldn't comprehend. I trusted my husband completely and that was a miracle. We were doing life and fighting battles together as partners the way God intended us. I became pregnant with our fifth child, a little boy, and he was such a gift. In my heart I knew God had added to our family in so many ways, and I loved everything about it. I thought everything was finally going to be okay.

I wish this was the high point of our journey. I wish I could tell a beautiful story of a battle with porn, sex, abuse, going from addiction to freedom, and ending with a beautiful little child. I wish I could tell about the perfect family of seven effortlessly serving the Lord in various ways and living happily ever after. It's what my social media shouted. It's what my face portrayed. It's what I honestly and genuinely wanted with every ounce of my being. It is what I tried to force into reality. But the truth is, I didn't feel this way at all. The honest reality is that this is not what my children experienced at all. What I desired in my heart is in no way where our journey was taking us. With childbirth came stress and my physical changes that required healing and adjusting. Adjustment did not go well, and distance began to creep in. Confrontation, arguing, and soon an emotional disconnect had come between my husband and me. I dropped from part time at my job at the hospital to "as needed." I attempted to meet the needs of our family in better ways. I kept thinking I had to be stronger. I had to protect my kids and my husband's ministry. If I could endure, my husband could minister. After all, we are never promised easy. I could continue using my photography gift God gave me to take beautiful experiences to capture on camera and share with others. I could do it. I just had to try a little harder and keep smiling a little longer.

I had a good life. I had beautiful kids and a family, great friends, a secure job that I loved that also provided a solid income, freedom, and free time. With these benefits, I could endure anything. All it cost me was sex. Not even sex like before; now it was physically easy but emotionally disconnected sex. I couldn't explain the disconnect but it was more than my heart could handle. I started drinking on nights when I knew sex would probably take place to numb the emotional pain. I started escaping as well. Being at home was no longer peaceful or fun as he had again become verbally manipulative and controlling. The oldest two children had moved out and were busy with their own interests. The three younger ones and I would go hiking or sit by the river, or sometimes visit a playground for entertainment—anywhere but sitting around in that house. I prayed for real freedom because I felt anything but free.

Work life was evolving for me, too. I had always loved my job, but a couple of events took place at the hospital that shook me to the core, and I wanted out. On the baby floor we have beautiful days, but we also walk with families through the harshest nightmares. Normally we care for patients for a twelve-hour shift and then go home. Those that experience the most tragic of losses, however, you carry with you for a lifetime. Sometimes you bring home so much more than you ever intended. My passion was caring for mothers and babies, but we were getting pulled away to cover on other floors more often, which was difficult for me because it was not what I signed up to do. I knew the Lord was nudging me, but I wasn't exactly sure how.

There are certain altar points I experienced in my faith journey. Many of us do and we look back on them and know that the Lord was speaking. Even if we don't know how or exactly what He is saying, we know that He is drawing us, calling out to us. With so much confusion in my head, I took my present life, my determination to hang on, my lack of contentment in my job, and concerns for close friends, along with my Bible, and headed to the woods alone where the Lord could speak to my heart through His creation. I strung up a hammock not knowing what I'd read. I opened my Bible to the book of James, "If you lack wisdom ask God . . . blessed is the man who perseveres for once he has been approved he will receive a crown . . . putting aside all filthiness and all of the remains of wickedness in humility receive the word implanted which is able to save your souls . . . the effective prayer of a righteous man can accomplish much . . . "

I asked for wisdom. I asked for direction. I asked to help resist temptation during the testing because I wanted so desperately to persevere. I also wish I could say that I learned from previous experiences and valiantly persevered; that I got rid of all wickedness and prayed continually. I failed at it all. It took a year to leave the hospital, and then about four months after that before I finally committed to a new job at a non-profit crisis pregnancy center in our area. Under the supervision of an OB/GYN who served as the Medical Director, I was trained to provide limited ultrasounds to our expectant moms so that they could see and bond with their babies. I was also trained to provide some of the parenting education classes for clients, and it just so happened that part of the training was related to recognizing abusive relationships. I swallowed hard as I looked at the "Power and Control" wheel for the first time, hoping no one noticed. Just about every spoke of that wheel applied to my marriage. I knew, though, that my husband was a minister and my family and children depended on my ability to withstand this marriage. At this point, I still believed that God had put me in this relationship, and that He would give me outlets in other ways along with strength to endure. I clung to the hope that one day He would grant freedom. I told myself that He would. After all, He is faithful. I told myself my outlets were okay, and I continued to attempt to be strong but *in my own strength*. At the same time, I talked to our clients and encouraged them to do what's right, and let God take care of the pieces.

With each client that faced serious circumstances, I began to feel more and more conviction. After my personal attempts at secrecy and cover ups, I can completely empathize with someone walking into a clinic for an abortion because it seems in the moment to be the easiest option. They can hide the evidence, go about life as normal, and tell themselves they will deal with the consequences of their decisions later. The battle is in the mind. If a person is strong enough to sustain the thoughts in her mind, she can terminate the "problem" and live life normal in appearance. It makes sense. I get it. The fear of an outward changed life is so very real. Fear will cause us to think all sorts of thoughts we never thought possible. However, our minds were never meant to live that way and we can't run from the emotional impact through silence and simply numb the pain. Our minds weren't meant to carry such heavy burdens alone. Jesus tells us He will give us rest. Matthew 11:28-30 talks about rest for our souls that is only found through Him. I knew this. If we do what's right and allow God to do the work that only He can do, we will find a peace that surpasses all understanding. He promises this in Philippians 4:7. "And the peace of God, which transcends all understanding, will guard your hearts and your minds in Christ Jesus." I told my clients this but telling it to myself was a different story. I was stronger. I could continue to numb myself to the sex and continue to escape and neglect my house by running off somewhere, seeking outlets that seemed healthy but were not. I could continue the façade and just keep going. No need to rock the boat. But God wants our heart. If our heart is neglecting to deal with sin, *refusing* to deal with sin, even the healthy things we do to numb the pain become part of the problem. I don't even remember what happened the night I prayed the prayer I shared earlier from my journal. I just know my husband and I weren't getting along and I went outside and prayed to God, admitting that I could not do this anymore. I had followed Him where I felt He was leading by giving up my self-supporting hospital job, remaining committed to my husband, and taking this job at a non-profit ministry. But I could not do this anymore. I would give up the drinking, I would give up the running, I would give up my outlets and trust Him, but I simply could not do this anymore. I needed God to fix this.

My husband never even knew that I had taken that time outside alone or that I had prayed that prayer. Three weeks later while he was out of town, I was sitting with my youngest son looking up YouTube videos of trains for him to watch on the iPad my husband had left behind for him to play on. Out of nowhere an email to my husband flashed across the screen from someone wanting to chat and hook up that weekend. I snapped a picture of the message with my phone and went to click his email to see if there were more, but it was already gone. Apparently, he had deleted the email using his phone. But I had the picture I had taken, and I sent him a text telling him I knew about the message, but I wasn't ready to talk about it yet. I sarcastically tossed out that I had the number if he needed it for the weekend. In that moment I was devastated, but honestly, I already knew. I had sensed that something was wrong, but I just didn't know exactly what. In my prayer I had given it all back to God. I hadn't had a drop to drink or run to my escape in three weeks, and here was my answer.

You pray and hope for an answer, but when it finally comes, the answer can be a difficult thing. It then becomes a choice as to what to do with the answer. Our oldest boy was graduating from the Air Force, and we had planned a family trip to see him. I had managed to endure circumstances this long, so

I decided to remain quiet and make the trip for the sake of the kids while thinking through my next steps and creating a plan of action for when we returned home. I encouraged my husband to talk to someone, and he agreed that he would when we got home. The kids knew nothing, and we had a great trip, although I knew that things would be so different in just a few days. I took a photo of my little girl dancing in the kitchen, my boys playing on the Switch, my husband doing the dishes, and while you can't see them in the photo, my oldest and youngest were playing trains on the floor. I sent it to friends to show that we were all together, celebrating four days in the perfect little temporary home we created in a vacation rental house. We finally had to say goodbye to our son, and the rest of us set out on the two-day trip back to our life in our real house and the real world.

As an introvert I love being away from crowds and my photographer side loves to experience the sky as far away from light pollution as possible, so we stayed at different state parks along the path to home, allowing us to enjoy nature and have greater privacy. I remember my husband lying in bed that last morning before we would arrive at home. I told him I wanted to get up and photograph the stars and then watch the sunrise. My husband knew that I knew his secrets, he knew what I loved, and he knew what stirred my heart. And as the alarm sounded, I got out of bed hoping that just maybe he would reveal some desire for the affection of my heart by making the effort to join me. But instead, he simply lay there. I walked out to the lake feeling so alone, wishing that he had exhibited some spark of desire or made some effort to join me that would indicate to me that he cared. I took photos of the beautiful scenery while I prayed for the strength to give up life as I knew it. I had seen the ugly hard truth, and I now had the clarity I needed. I knew I could not hide anymore.

The weeks that followed are now a blur. I was aware that things had reached a point where action could quickly cause the situation to become unsafe. But I didn't back down as I called for help, and as help came confrontation took place. The word *failure* was again in the forefront of my mind as I pulled my children out of their beds in the middle of the night and left our house. *How did I let things get to this point?* I thought to myself.

Almost two days after that confrontation, my husband made a step in the right direction by resigning his position as a minister. While it was the right choice, when the resignation was final, my heart was so heavy. There was no turning back. What I had feared and given every part of my being for the past eight years to avoid was quickly becoming a reality. Fourteen years of marriage, eight years of living with the awareness of his addiction, eight years of fighting this battle with all that I had, and yet, life was still falling apart. There would be no keeping things quiet anymore. We lived in a small community and our lives were about to go public. I was terrified. My children, his ministry, life as we knew it . . . The fears were so real, and I was overwhelmed. I had a very real moment of complete terror. I could not do this; I could not walk this road. Had I been given the option I might have done everything in my power to make it all disappear. But clearer than I've ever before seen in my mind, I saw Jesus walking on water, holding out his hand . . . "I've got this, I've got you," He said to me. "Keep your eyes on me, don't pay attention to the waves, don't pay attention to the storm, keep your eyes on me, keep your focus."

Was it audible? No. Did I listen? Momentarily, yes, but overall, no, not really. I was still terrified. Regardless though, I know that I heard Him and saw Him in my mind. I know He sent those words to give comfort, and even if my faith struggled, the comfort was real. I knew that He never meant for me to do this alone.

Through the wisdom I have gained along this journey, I no longer believe as I did in my younger years that viewing pornography is no big deal. At the time of this writing, my family and I are living out the reality of the destruction caused by pornography. My husband is enrolled at a treatment center in another state for nine months as he is attempting to renew and heal his mind. I have no idea what his next steps will be after that program. My oldest son is still in the Air Force, stationed in another state. His sacrifice to serve our country helped prepare us for the distance our family would experience on this journey. It also provided me with a means of explaining to our children what it sometimes takes to equip, train in discipline, and train in battle. In my son's particular branch of the military, he had eight weeks of basic training (boot camp) where he learned discipline, retrained his mind, retrained his focus and default coping skills, and learned to depend on the proven and trusted standards set in place. After his graduation from basic training he was then sent to another base where he spent three months learning a trade and specific skill that would equip him for battle. His job is specific, and he has been equipped for a specific task, but in the big picture, he works with a crew of people for a common goal. The Air Force is also just a single branch of our military that works with other branches for the common goal of protecting our country and fighting for worthy causes. We are *the body of believers* called "according to a purpose" as noted in Romans 8:28. I explained to our children that daddy's absence was similar to their big brother's because daddy was going to a place where he would learn to retrain his mind so that hopefully he would be safe to be around.

My oldest daughter works in another city, and my younger children and I are continuing to do life, and to adjust to a home with just the four of us. Our family dynamic has changed so much these past few months, and we are adjusting to our new reality. I'm sure there have been far worse consequences related to pornography that we have not had to endure just as there are surely other stories that do not require quite this extent of action to overcome. I fully believe God equips us individually for the journey.

So, what is my purpose in sharing this story? I understand the fear. I'm living in the middle of it. There are moments where I've wanted to turn back, too, and go back to the bondage, go back to the slavery, go back where things were "normal" and secure. That isn't freedom though. The Israelites longed for Egypt as well, but they were headed to the promised land. The wilderness is dry and difficult. Sometimes it seems to have no end. But even in the wilderness He still provides. In the wilderness the Israelites' clothes and shoes did not wear out (Deuteronomy 29:5). And in the wilderness, the Israelites were not able to see the end of their journey. They couldn't see, but in Deuteronomy chapter 30, God explains that He will restore for those who turn to Him. He frees from bondage, and in 31:8 He states that "the Lord himself goes before you and will be with you; he will never leave you nor forsake you. Do not be afraid; do not be discouraged."

"The Lord himself goes before you . . . " It brings me to tears even now. He is guiding this journey. I know I have felt His peace that passes understanding in the darkest of circumstances. Our family looks different, but we are still here, still surviving, and I still see the Lord working in my life. I cling to His promises. I cling to the fact that doing what's right will be blessed. I've done everything I can think of to survive on my own, to numb the pain, to fill the void, while professing Christ the entire time. There is no denying we are spiritual and emotional beings. I believe I was just as much a Christian when I accepted Jesus as my Lord and Savior at age nine as I am now, but that doesn't mean I've always chosen the right path. It doesn't mean I've always felt Him with me, and it doesn't mean I've always believed. I mess it up all the time, but I know there has been growth. I know my heart is seeking the right path. And I know that seeking the right path is so much more peaceful than numbing your heart to the wrong one. There is still fear, but my heart has experienced more freedom now than ever before. I know I don't want to go anywhere where He Himself hasn't gone before me, and I know that I can honestly encourage you to do the same.

It is okay not to know the ending. It's okay not to see. The Lord carries us through until He sets us on another path, and He doesn't always reveal where we are headed. He doesn't have to because if we are allowing Him to lead, we can rest in the assurance that He knows the way. He goes before us.

It doesn't mean it is easy and it doesn't even mean healing will take place this side of heaven. In fact, I know complete restoration cannot happen on earth. That is what makes my hope in heaven so real. My job is having faith until He provides clarity and closure. My job is to battle where He has placed and equipped me. Even now when I look at that power and control wheel, I know my husband still reacts abusively in phone calls. How am I supposed to believe in healing when the evidence of illness is written in black and white? With the faith of a mustard seed, that's how. I remember the goodness of the Father, I trust in His equipping for battle, I trust His timing, and I trust that He will guide this path my family is on. I've seen His blessings in the journey up to this point. I know without a doubt I do not want to take a single step without Him, and that has been one of the biggest gifts of my experiences. The ability to believe even when everything screams not to is also a gift, even if the battle plan doesn't make sense. Even if I'm asked to march around a wall seven times and never see a single piece of the wall crumble like Jericho, or if God leads me to what appears to be a dead end at a body of water with a massive army behind me without a single ripple or hint of parting in the Red Sea, it is not my job to take control out of fear. He will work a miracle. He will give clarity, or He will give closure, and I must hang on in belief. It is not within my own understanding, and I can take comfort that because I am His, when I follow Him, I know I'm headed toward the promised land. "Do not let your hearts be distressed. You believe in God; believe also in me. There are many dwelling places in my Father's house. Otherwise, I would have told you, because I am going away to make ready a place for you. And if I go and make ready a place for you, I will come again and take you to be with me, so that where I am you may be too" (John 14:1-3 NET). And because His love is perfect, He has sent a helper until that time comes (also in chapter 14).

Our family could use your prayers. I have five precious children that mean the world to me and they are all at various stages of healing and dealing with life's circumstances. I have a husband who longs for true freedom. I long for freedom as well. I long to be all that the Lord has purposed for me to be. I have personally prayed for those that will encounter this book. I pray that our stories and our willingness to break the silence will take away some of the loneliness that exists in quiet struggles. The apostle Paul felt the loneliness when he said, "At my first defense, no one came to my support, but everyone deserted me" (2 Timothy 4:16). But then comes the beautiful verse that follows. "But the Lord stood at my side and gave me strength, so that through me the message might be fully proclaimed."

I have been blessed with the right people in my life at the right time. However, loneliness has still been so prevalent. My prayer is that even in the darkest moments may you feel the Lord by your side. We are not alone, and we all have stories, a "message" of victory that the Lord has given us. It truly is a hard and narrow road to walk (Matt 7:14). But great are the rewards and great is the peace that passes all understanding. My family still has joy. We still have life. We still love to laugh. God is good and is walking with our family one moment at a time. I believe with all my heart that He will do the same for you and yours if you choose to break free from the sin that "so easily entangles" as we remember that we have a "great cloud of witnesses" surrounding us (Hebrews 12:1). He's got this!

CHAPTER 7

Longing for Home

My husband and I had been married twelve years when we discovered we were pregnant with our fifth child. Our first four children were stairsteps born one right after the other, and the youngest would be starting kindergarten in the fall. We thought that our family was complete with the four, but obviously God had other plans.

We had just finished a major remodel on our home, and I was well on my way to having it just like I wanted it. Adding another baby to the mix, however, meant that the house simply wasn't going to be big enough. We needed more room. I was all for staying put and building an addition onto the back, but my husband thought that it would look out of place with the layout and the style of the house, so he contrived a moving plan. We had an elderly neighbor who was moving into an apartment and my husband had talked with her about the possibility of buying her house. Her property joined the back side of ours, so he wanted to buy her house which was bigger than our current home and move us there. It was actually going to be a temporary arrangement because the bigger picture that he had in mind was to subdivide the properties once they were joined together in our name and then sell the land to someone who might want to develop a new subdivision, or to subdivide the land himself and sell it. Then we would be set to purchase a forever home that would hold our growing family.

During this planning, when I was about sixteen weeks pregnant, we gathered up the kids and took a family trip to the beach. This was the first time that we had braved a family vacation without taking an extra helper along. We arrived and I went right to work getting the condo stocked with food items and unpacking so that we could have some fun. The second day was our first full day on the beach. We ate breakfast and went down to the ocean for a little while, and then walked back up to the condo for a bite of lunch and a bathroom break. We watched the movie *Miracle* while we ate, and I felt a little discomfort that was comparable to light cramping. I took a Tylenol and went about getting things packed up to head back down to the beach. As I sat on the shore, watching the kids and my husband play in the water, I felt a sudden gush of fluid. I stood up quickly, calling for my husband as I realized I had blood running down my legs.

He hurriedly got us all back up to the room where we called the local hospital emergency room and asked them if we should come in. My husband told the doctor approximately how much blood we thought I had passed, and then proceeded to explain that we had gone through a similar experience a few years before during my third pregnancy. We were nineteen and a half weeks along with that baby, and I ended up losing our daughter to premature delivery. Here we were with no family or friends to help us, and we were afraid that we were about to relive the same terrible nightmare that we had experienced before.

The doctor told my husband to take me to the emergency room so that I could be monitored, and we buckled up the kids and hurried on our way. I was whisked quickly to the back and my husband was left to handle the little ones and run interference with the doctors as well. It wasn't long before they determined that I had experienced a partial placental abruption. They filled my husband in on the details and potential risks but decided it was best for the health of the baby and me if they didn't tell me everything just yet. The decision was made to transfer me to a nearby women's and children's hospital that could better care for our needs, and they transported me there by ambulance. I remember having such an unusual calmness in my spirit, and I knew that God was with me. I prayed as they were unloading me from the ambulance, telling God that whatever purpose He had in allowing this, I knew that it was going to be okay. I prayed that He would help me to handle things in a way that would bring Him glory.

It wasn't long before the staff had me in a curtained area undergoing an ultrasound. The technician didn't look very happy and the doctor showed up shortly after to provide more details and to fill me in on my options. Ultimately the diagnosis was grim and life-threatening to both my baby and me. He informed me of the placental abruption and told me that if the tear continued and the placenta tore completely away, I could bleed out in a matter of minutes and the baby would die as well. The solution he offered and strongly suggested that I take was to terminate the pregnancy. He told me that my other four children needed their mother and that although he was a pro-life doctor, in a case like mine, this was what he recommended.

I just remember feeling so strangely calm and honestly not upset at all. I looked at that doctor and asked him, "If I make this decision, even if I live, *how can I live with myself?*" I proceeded to tell him that I understood the risks, but that I would not terminate my pregnancy. This baby was a gift from God, and I would carry it until God either chose to take me or to deliver my baby. I told him that I loved my children, but if God chose to take me home to heaven, then He would take care of them and place someone in their lives that would have something to offer them that maybe I didn't have to give. All I knew for sure was that I had to trust God in this. God gave me the strength to make that decision in those moments and not look back.

My husband supported my decision and so we began trying to figure out how to get back home so we could work our way through the rest of this experience. Many friends back home began praying, and close friends showed up to take my other four children back to the beach condo to pack up and take them back to their house with them. I surprised the doctors and nurses by showing rapid improvement in my blood pressure and other vitals, and after much coaxing, they released me to travel home on a path that kept me close to hospitals along the way. I was to go directly to my doctor the next morning to develop a plan of care.

Thankfully, the trip home was uneventful, and the next day I went to my obstetrician who then referred me to a local doctor who specialized in treating patients with high-risk pregnancies. It was Friday and I was given instructions to go home, stay off my feet completely, and to return to his office first thing Monday morning unless I saw him in the emergency room before. He gave no false hope, and I knew from sneaking a peek at the records I transferred to him from my regular doctor's office that there was an eighty percent or more chance that I was expected to lose this baby. Because we lived about an hour away from the hospital, that also meant that my life was at great risk as well. But again, the calmness came, and I knew that God was all in this situation. He gave me the strength to go on without fear of what could be.

The weekend was uneventful, and when we returned to the specialist on Monday, the doctor told us that he was shocked that he hadn't seen us over the weekend in the ER. An ultrasound showed that the tear hadn't gotten any worse, so while we weren't out of the woods, we appeared to be holding our own. Only time would tell. I was instructed to go home, stay off my feet, and to get up only to go to the restroom and take a quick shower after which I was to immediately go back to sitting or lying down again. I was told to schedule a weekly appointment unless I saw any sign of bleeding, at which point I was to call and get to the hospital immediately.

But there was nothing. No spotting, no bleeding. The pregnancy continued, and baby and I both did fine. As difficult as it was with four little children to care for, we made it work. Friends brought meals, gave rides to school, and helped clean our house. My husband worked his job and did the laundry when he got home. I did find it somewhat humorous that during his season of laundry duty he decided that we needed a bigger washing machine and proceeded to purchase one right away.

I honestly don't know exactly when it took place, but somewhere in the chaos, we moved into the neighbor's house that I mentioned before. My husband moved my recliner into the new living room, and it was from that vantage point that I sat and pointed and gave directions for the items coming through the doors as friends and family moved us in. It wasn't until probably two years later that I found things my husband had hidden in the barn because he was tired of moving and just wanted to put an end to the mess and keep me off my feet. I had to remind myself in those moments that he was on overload and trying to help, and that things were just things and could be replaced. With the journey that lay ahead, that was a valuable lesson to keep in mind.

The pregnancy went on like this for one month, then two, and after the third month, I was given the all clear and released to go back to normal activities. We were going to be okay. I was relieved to share this news with our oldest daughter especially, since she hadn't been very excited about adding another sibling from the very beginning. Maybe the extra hormones of pregnancy had made me more sensitive to her lack of excitement. But I realized that even when we are walking in obedience to God's plan everybody else around us may not be as excited about it as we are.

Any reservations anyone had about a new baby were laid to rest once the baby arrived and was handed off to be passed around and loved on. It was my fifth child, after all, so I was way past panicking over germs or fear of someone dropping her. My little girls who were in kindergarten and first grade had practiced their skills on their baby dolls in preparation, and they were ready to tackle the real deal. I kept an eye on them, of course, but I let them enjoy mothering her. They combed her hair, dressed her up, and rocked her to their heart's content. I loved watching them fall in love with her. My oldest daughter started calling her "my baby," and my son rocked her and held her right along with the girls. This baby had it made. She was good-natured, loved the attention, and was a wonderful addition to our crew.

About this time the economy was taking a big nose-dive, and my husband's work was greatly affected which meant that our income took a hit as well. Things were tight with the expense of owning two homes, along with our growing family expenses. I was a stay-at-home mom since childcare would have cost us more than I would have ever made with a salary. Being home to raise my children was a privilege, but I am a driven woman, so it was also difficult for me to sacrifice the pursuit of a career. I made friends and kept myself busy, but with a tight income, there was no extra money. Staying home meant entertaining myself and our kids with free activities that were close to home in order to conserve gas. My one splurge was a weekly trek to Community Bible Study where my kids and I loved the people, lessons, and interaction.

Those were difficult days. With so many children, somebody was always in need of something, and with the decrease in our income we struggled to provide. Gone were the vacation and condo days, as basic needs had become all we could meet. Then another surprise came as I found out that I was pregnant with baby number six. Everything went smoothly this time throughout the pregnancy right up until the moment of delivery. However, right after my water broke during labor, I had a full placental abruption, and I began to hemorrhage. I barely remember being told what had happened, because the hospital staff knocked me out immediately and I had an emergency C-section within moments. Once again, the doctors and nurses fought to save both mine and my baby's lives. Praise God, my baby girl made it here safely. And I guess you figured since I wrote this chapter for the book, that I, too, made it. However, I think my baby girl had something to say about the stressful way in which she came into this world. For her first year of life, she cried without stopping. She literally drove me and everyone around our family crazy. Between her unpleasant disposition and caring for five other children, I was completely overwhelmed.

I went into a depression that was related to more than postpartum that lasted for several years. I felt defeated financially, and I struggled to parent kids entering the unchartered territory of teenage years. I had to learn how to navigate boyfriends, vehicles, insurance, and wardrobes while trying to make ends meet with a constantly crying baby on my shoulder. It was difficult, to say the least. One day, while the kids and I were visiting with my mother-in-law, she told me that these were the best years of my life. Later at home I cried and told my husband that if this was the best my life was ever going to be, then I didn't know *what* I was going to do. (Thankfully we are in a place where we laugh about that now.)

I remember praying one day when I was at my lowest. I got down on my knees in front of the chair where I usually sat to rock my babies. It was beside a window and the curtains were open on that overcast day. I asked God for miracles and His provision. I suddenly noticed the warmth of sunshine and soft rays falling across my face as the clouds parted. I felt His presence. I knew in my spirit that He had heard me, and that the sun *was* going to shine again. I didn't know when and I didn't know how, but somehow God gave me a peace that it was all going to be okay.

My husband worked harder than he had ever worked before. He had always worked long hours at his job, but it was an office job where he dressed in slacks and did desk work, sales, and talked. As his salary had taken hit after hit, he finally left the office with its long hours, and began a yard and tree trimming business. Our son who was entering his teen years worked by my husband's side. That time my son got to work so closely with his daddy was one of the most positive things that occurred. My husband is a hard worker, and he taught my son to work hard and to work with integrity. We may have been poor, but I was proud of my son, and I knew that my husband did all he could do to provide; it just took more than most families for us to survive because we had such a large brood. But still, I wouldn't have traded any of them for anything.

We had a garden, so I cooked with the food we grew, and we ate well enough. At times groceries appeared on our doorsteps, or friends showed up with hand-me-down clothes as the seasons changed. It sometimes felt like everybody knew our struggle, but I later learned that very few people did. During this time, I also cooked for the family of one of my daughter's friends. The mom hired me to prepare dinner for their family just as I was preparing for mine. She wasn't the homemaker type, so this allowed her family to have a homecooked meal. I also cleaned house for my sister-in-law who drove an hour both ways to work a full-time job and managed life as a single parent to her two teenage children. She ran constantly between her job and their practices and games. I needed the money and she, like my other friend, needed the help, so it was a good solution for both of us. However, it still pricked what little bit of pride I had left. I recall a day that I was scrubbing the toilets in her home, asking God if this was the best He had for me—a college graduate, cleaning people's toilets. He gave me a different perspective. He reminded me that by cleaning those toilets I was serving my sister-in-law who had been up since the wee hours of the morning preparing things for her children's day, answering to the responsibilities of her job, and then driving back home to cook supper and continue to fulfill her duties as a mom. Then she would lay her head down on her pillow that night, all alone, to sleep and then start the process all over again the next day. I imagined how it would feel to her after the activities of her day to walk into a home that smelled clean and fresh and where she hadn't had to do a thing because someone had served *her* for a change. I was suddenly okay with scrubbing her toilets. Only God can change your heart like that!

Gradually, we began to pay our debts. It was tight, but we worked hard, and God rewarded our efforts. As we were recovering financially, I spent many tearful days in the house that was supposed to have been our temporary dwelling, longing to sell the property as we had originally planned and move into a place that would feel more like home. But with the dip in the economy, those plans were no longer an option. To keep our finances afloat we sold off our old home and part of the land. It was a difficult choice, and as I looked out of my kitchen window across the field to our old house every day and relived in my mind the good times that we'd had there before hardship hit, our current situation looked even more bleak. As always seems to happen when finances are tight, things around the place broke or needed to be replaced, but there was no extra money to invest in repairs. Over time the wear and tear on the house began to show from the people that lived there and the friends they brought home. The house looked as worn out as I did. I thought we could both use a facelift, and I did my best to make the house inviting for friends and family. I would pray for God to help us afford a home, not just a house to live in, and then I would repent immediately for being materialistic. It was such an emotional struggle! I longed to entertain, to have a comfortable place to host a life group or to entertain friends who might need someone to minister to them, but the house was worn, the space was small, and the furniture was a mess. *But . . .* the children who lived there and caused the wear and tear in that home and made things such a mess? They were precious and loved, and I knew that they were my true treasures from God. I was reminded of it every time I read Proverbs 24:4: "Through knowledge its rooms are filled with rare and beautiful treasures." I was thankful that God had given me the ability to see children as a blessing from Him, but it was still so confusing to me as I tried to balance gratefulness for my blessings with the reality of the needs we were struggling to meet. This was a battle that lasted for seven long years, and emotionally I was as worn out as my home and my hand-me-down belongings looked.

By now my babies were growing up and playing sports. I was at one of their volleyball games and made an offhand comment to a friend about her beautiful home. She is a teacher with a servant's heart that looks after the needs of many, and she also ministered to my high school-age girls, so I was truly happy that she had been blessed with such a beautiful home. She responded with a laugh and told me that it was totally a God thing that they were in that home. I prompted her to tell me more, and she proceeded to tell me about all that God had done and the miracles that He had performed to bring them to the perfect home for which she had prayed for many years. She talked about her journey and her battle with desiring a home yet feeling materialistic, but then realizing that God knew the desires of her heart and longed to bless her in that way. Her words went straight to my heart and tears began to roll down my cheeks right there in the bleachers as I listened to her story. When she finished, I told her that I had been praying for God to provide me with a home, too! I had a house, but I wanted a *home* that would be a place of comfort and hope and that would have fresh memories and new opportunities. My friend lovingly told me that she understood exactly what I meant, that I was not being materialistic, and that she would pray for God to show me the home that He had for me.

When my youngest child was four, I took a brave step and accepted God's call to a job at a ministry I loved. It offered the flexibility that I needed with my family's schedule, and I enrolled my four-year-old in preschool and went to work. I loved the challenge but it was a stressful job, and as I added the responsibility to my efforts of maintaining our busy household, there was a need for a place that felt like home to refresh and renew from all that I had to do each day. I asked God to guide me and told Him that I was ready to take the leap of faith and begin actively looking for my home as if I believed that He really would provide one, just as He had done for my friend. I would get in my car when I had a free moment and ask God for directions as I buckled up. I had given Him a few specific things I wanted, and with those parameters in mind, I drove around and looked for a house that fit the description. It had to be close to school since my children played sports, and I had to request help with rides due to work. The economy had experienced a little boost, and my husband had taken a good job offer in his old profession, so our home needed to have land where he could still ride his tractor, which was his outlet after a hard day at work. It also needed to be spacious since our house was always full of people and late-night visitors that I didn't want to be sitting right outside of my bedroom door watching TV and talking while I was trying to go to sleep at night. And oh yes, bathrooms . . . we had to have *lots* of bathrooms with our houseful of girls!

My oldest daughter had recently met her love, and they were ready to get married. It was a wonderful time in life, as I had watched her become a young woman and saw the man that God had been preparing for her for her entire life. She is my peaches and cream, blond-haired, blue-eyed beauty, and her whole life she had loved "form people" as she would say when she was little, referring to "foreign" people. She loved dark hair, dark eyes, and dark skin, which was her complete opposite. She had dated a few guys, but none of them fit that description. Then one day, out of the blue when she was having lunch with my husband in between college classes, this handsome young man appeared at the Mexican restaurant where they were eating. She paid no attention to his attempts to catch her eye while they were eating, and in a final attempt to get her number, he ran out to the parking lot, caught up to them as they were headed for their cars, and asked her daddy if he could ask her for her number. Her daddy told her she was old enough to decide for herself, and that is how their love story began. Now, a year and a half later, my husband called a local bed and breakfast that also served as a wedding venue to inquire about the cost of having the wedding at their facility. The owner told him that due to health problems, they were no longer renting it as a venue, and were considering selling the property. My husband had always loved the place and told them that if they ever decided that they were going to sell it, he would love to know. He told me about the conversation later, and I was totally against the idea, saying it was more than we could afford or maintain. He pled his case a little more, but the house didn't fit my perfect description, so with a resounding no, I marked it off the list, and continued to drive around every so often in search of our perfect home.

One night, I stayed up after everyone else had gone to bed. It was a rare moment when I had the TV all to myself and could watch anything that I pleased. I turned on a Beth Moore series that I had recorded and began to lean in for a word of encouragement. She taught on the longings of our heart and about how God Himself had designed us to have those longings. She said that they weren't wrong or materialistic and then she asked very specifically, "What are you longing for?"

It was as if she were speaking directly to me, and as she paused, I found myself answering out loud, "I'm longing for a home!"

As soon as the words fell from my mouth, I realized that the name of the bed and breakfast my husband had spoken to me about was "Longing for Home." I sat there a little shocked, resigning myself to the fact that I at least had to go and give the property a look.

The next day the owners graciously allowed us to come and view the inside of the house. From the moment I set eyes on the staircase it felt like home. In my mind I could see my kids running up and down those stairs into the spacious rooms and open floorplan. My list of requirements was met, along with so many extras! I thanked God repeatedly for His goodness and faithfulness to me, and to this day, as I walk up the driveway pulling a trash can after garbage day, or as I sit on my front porch and listen to the birds singing in the beautiful tree-filled yard, I thank Him for blessing me with a home and for giving me the desires of my heart. It amazes me that it is not only just what I wanted but so much more. If this is the kind of home He gives me here on earth, I can't imagine what heaven will be like in all its perfect beauty!

One last thing—okay, two things. First, remember that the answers to my prayers didn't always come quickly. Healing during my pregnancy took several months, the right man to be my daughter's husband was prayed over for years, deliverance from financial struggles also took years, and it took years to see the home that I longed for become a reality. I want to encourage you not to give up. Keep praying and talking to God about your needs and the desires of your heart. Ask Him to help your desires line up with what will bring Him the most glory, and I believe that you will see answers to your prayers come to fruition.

Second, I want to talk a little more about how my home has prepared me for heaven. I realize that this home is just a temporary dwelling. I know that anything could happen at any time and this home might not be mine anymore. But I'm okay with that, because God has given me a small peek at what heaven will be like in giving me this home. Don't misunderstand me. I love living here, but my love for my home (which is by no means fancy or perfect) is made so much greater because I know that it was a place that He prepared for me, and I can only imagine how He smiled as He saw my tears of joy and appreciation for His gift! I really think He loved move-in day as much as I did. If He was so good as to prepare this earthly place for me that meets my needs and even more, then I can barely begin to imagine what heaven will be like. In John 14 Jesus explained to His disciples that He must leave them for a time, as He told them that He was going to prepare a place for them in His Father's house, which has many rooms. He also told them that He would one day come again and take them to be with Him. I believe this with all of my heart. I believe that He will come and take His children to the forever home that He has been busy preparing for them.

So, my question for you is this: are you His child? If you are unsure, or if you would say, "No," I would encourage you to read the final chapter in this book to learn more about this heavenly home and what a relationship with Christ could look like for you. I truly hope that one day you will choose Him, and that we might enjoy His heavenly home together!

CHAPTER 8

Pure White

White walls, white ceilings, white lab coats. White paper littering the nurse's desks . . . White surrounded me. It had never been my favorite color. Since I was a little girl there was just something about white that didn't sit well with me. Maybe it was the fact that it had such potential to be so easily stained and flawed, or maybe I found it annoying in all its perfection. Whatever the reason, I was now surrounded by it during one of the most horrific experiences of my life.

My incredible family made growing up easy. I feel like every time someone decides to seek therapy some of the first questions asked are, "What was your home life like? Did you have a stable environment growing up?" The answer to both of those questions is a resounding "Yes!" However, one thing you need to know about Satan is that he finds loopholes. He finds the cracks in the foundation. He seeks out our vulnerable areas and when they are exposed, he attacks them ruthlessly even when things appear on the outside to be two thumbs up.

My daddy: one of the greatest examples of a provider and God-fearing leader of a household that I have ever known. He is also one of the most self-sacrificing individuals I know. There were many birthdays, holidays, basketball games, voice recitals, and church services he had to miss through the years to bring home a steady source of income to support his family. I love my daddy. One of my fondest memories to this day is that while I was growing up, I would know it would be about time to head out for wherever we were going when I heard him playing the piano. It was *always* the old hymn, "There Is a Fountain." Those sweet notes filled our home and burrowed their way into my heart.

My mom: my angel, my best friend. She has been through the darkest parts of my life with me and always brought her flashlight. She has always been there to uplift and encourage my soul. I truly wish that there were parts of my story that she had not had to walk through with me because I know it was rough on her. She has always been there to tell me everything would be all right. I don't know what I did to deserve her, but I couldn't be more thankful that I get to call her mine. I am a carbon copy of her. Everything from my super slow southern accent all the way to how we just don't use common sense sometimes. I like to think of it as an endearing quality.

My little brother: the athlete, the goofball, the kid with a heart of gold. I was six years old when he was born and made our little family complete. I stared into those big blue eyes, and I was hooked from the start. I'm still under his spell even after twenty-one years. He has such a servant's heart and does all that he can when he knows things need to be done. He prefers to serve behind the scenes, and has never been one that needed the spotlight or a pat on the back for a job well done. He loves like Jesus and does what he thinks will please the Lord. I have never had to worry about him and his decision-making. Unlike his big sister, he seems to have things a little more together than I did when I was his age.

I felt like it was important for you to know the people that helped raise me to prove that I wasn't lying when I said I grew up with a good home life. I guess it's time now for me to start unraveling the scroll and tell my part of the story. It's not a pretty little testimony all wrapped up in shiny paper with a big red bow tied on top, but then again, I guess that's what makes it beautiful. The fact that God takes our ugly and turns it into lovely for His glory.

Long, curly brown hair and a desire to make people laugh pretty much sums me up as a little girl. Both of my parents grew up a bit reserved and shy, especially when they were kids, so I've often asked my parents where my personality came from. My mother to this day still smiles brightly, shakes her head, and simply states, "You are just what I ordered." That spunky little personality lasted a few years, but it didn't take long in my life for Satan to start creeping in and slowly making me feel valued less with each passing year. I was about five years old when a little excess baby fat started to make me feel ugly. I know the picture I had of myself was untrue, a lie from Satan, as I look back now on old albums and see that I was a normal, healthy sized little girl. There was nothing monstrous or disgusting about the way I looked.

As I began kindergarten not much changed. I had friends and liked everything that school consisted of for the most part. It was not until I was in the third grade that I really started noticing that I was bigger than the other girls my age. I would say ten percent of that awareness was self-observation and the other ninety was through the giggles and name calling that came from the other kids. I was reminded pretty much daily from the girls in my class how different I looked. I remember being mooed at like a cow and my seat being taken and my stuff moved when I would leave the lunchroom table for a second. I wish I could say that I handled it well. I wish I could tell you that I let it all roll off my back, but that was not the case. I turned now to food more than ever for comfort. I had always had a personality that was so outgoing. Yet, the more my weight became an issue, the more I wanted to crawl in a shell and just pray that nobody would notice me.

One vivid memory I have is folding laundry as a child and slowly outgrowing my jeans. I remember them being a few sizes smaller than my mother's and then a few years later we were the same size. But what made my stomach turn most was when I was in pants that were a size bigger than hers. I was in the fifth grade. My mother has always been average in size. But Satan took the hatred that I had as I compared myself to my mother and ran with it until I was very overweight and very miserable. Middle school was probably the start of some of the unhealthiest years of my life from an emotional and mental standpoint. Comparison had completely taken my heart captive at this point. "Why can't I look like her?" "Why can't my hair be straight like that girl's?" "Why can't I just have a boyfriend?" The *whys* were not my friends.

In the seventh grade, I changed schools. I went from a public school setting to a private Christian school thinking that if I could just have a fresh start, all of my insecurities and all of the self-hatred I carried for myself would go away and there would be an awesome do-over. It was my experience that bullying was not tolerated as much in a private school, which was helpful, but the insecurities were still like a heavy fog in my spirit. The entire time I was in school I never had a boyfriend. Basically, every year that I did not have a boyfriend, from the point that I hit puberty on, I felt increasingly more as if something was wrong with me. I went through my entire middle and high school years with that mindset. I never felt good enough or worthy enough for someone of the opposite sex. I had friends both in and out of school. Most were in my youth group, and I was very much involved in church. I was always there: I went on every youth trip, sang specials, eventually was a small group leader, and even a Sunday school teacher. I felt like the biggest hypocrite every Sunday morning telling all those sweet girls about how they needed to value themselves while inside I despised my very existence. I let a boy I had been best friends with for years play with my heart and emotions. When that didn't work out and he went on to his next girlfriend, I felt like I truly had no value. There was nothing about me at that point that I thought was worth living for. My heart was broken and trying to put myself back together through my own efforts to recover was not a pretty picture.

I started going to a community college close to home and thought that maybe, just maybe, *this* could be my fresh start. I had another opportunity at my do-over. I made it to college and loved it. I had a scholarship for chorus and made lots of friends through my involvement there. I went to a few parties, drank a little, and had a little more freedom than in the past. I was in school for nursing until I got very sick about halfway through my first semester of classes. I was nauseated, dizzy, passing out, and suffering from extreme fatigue. I had to drop out of nursing school, which crushed me and made my self-worth tank emptier than it already was. My binge eating was out of control. I would eat huge amounts of food and then throw it up. This was the start of my eating disorder. Instead of fighting against this thing that had its grip on me, I would return frequently to the vice that had me entangled so tightly I couldn't breathe. I was in bed all the time. I felt awful. I remember one time trying to make myself purge in the bathroom. Food got caught in my throat and I thought I was choking. I remember being by myself and thinking I might die right there over the toilet.

I couldn't handle the reality of failure that had taken hold of my life. I started to become numb. I was so numb that my emotions and sense of reality were almost completely gone. I started making comments about my life like, "I wish I had never been born," and "My family's lives would be so much better without me in them." My mother, in all her motherly way, wouldn't accept those statements. She would scold me every time I uttered those words. However, despite the scolding, those statements became more and more frequent. I truly believed what I was saying. I thought of every word as fact. One day as I was lying in bed my mom came into my room and told me that we were going to the hospital. I remember not feeling anything as I got out of bed and loaded up into the car. I don't remember us speaking a word to each other the entire drive. I just remember thinking of different ways that I could end the numbness and the feeling of failure and defeat I felt in my soul.

We walked through the doors of the emergency room and I remember nothing other than my mom filling out paperwork. My name was called shortly after, and we made our way to a back room. I sat on the examination table with nothing but glazed eyes staring at the floors. The ER doctor came in and sounded like Charlie Brown's muffled teacher. I didn't hear a word he said until he got to this question: "Do you want your life to end?" I stared back at him with those glazed eyes and just nodded my head. The next question that followed was, "Do you want to be admitted into our unit?" All that could come to my mind was to ask, "Will they be able to help me?" He looked at me and not very convincingly said that they could. I agreed to be admitted and before I knew it, I was in a wheelchair going through lots of twists and turns, up elevators and down again. More turns followed until I landed at the registration desk of the hospital's psychiatric unit. The nurse left my mom and me with another lady where we would fill out more paperwork. If I had been thinking clearly and known fully what I was signing my name to on those sheets of paper, I would have run out of there without a second thought and never looked back.

We finished the paperwork and with a tearful goodbye, my mother hugged me and walked out of that unit hoping and praying that they could in some way provide the help I needed. I was escorted to my room and was told that once I was settled, I could go to the main living area and watch TV before lights out if I wanted. I remember setting my things down and walking out to where another man was on a couch watching *Family Feud*. I think it was the first time in my life I had sat and watched that show where there was no laughter. The only laughter that filled the room was echoing from the TV audience in the background. I was now in a place where laughter and joy had come to die. I looked more closely at the man and saw that he had a bandage wrapped around his neck. All I could think of was what was underneath that bandage, which was evidence of why he was in the unit to begin with. On that note, I made my way to bed early and shut my door. A nurse came to the door and opened it. "You are not allowed to shut your door. It's regulations," she explained.

I guess I could understand why that was a rule. We were in a psych ward, after all. That night I was awakened every two to three hours by the hospital staff so that they could take vitals and draw blood. I felt as though every time

I was able to settle down enough to fall asleep, someone would come in with stethoscopes and needles to start the process all over again.

The next morning, I groggily made my way to the main living area where this time more bodies filled the room. I saw a girl sitting on the couch that looked about my age and she seemed friendly. I sat by her and introduced myself. She reached out to shake my hand and I could see the deep red gash that ran the length of her entire arm. That gash was undoubtedly from an experience that required a visit to the emergency room. Fresh white bandages coated her other arm from her most recent attempt at taking her own life.

I, on the other hand, had never actually attempted anything. What made me slightly different from the others that filled the room was that at some point every one of them had attempted to end it all. You could see the bandages on them where that had been the case, all except for one man who had tried to drink a bottle of bleach and had to have his stomach pumped the night before. The common thread that bonded us together in that room were the feelings of being helpless, hopeless, and having no drive to keep going.

After a while, the hospital brought in a lady for therapy. In my opinion, she had a very outgoing and inappropriate disposition for someone you would bring in to help people who had recently tried to end their lives. She had us all in a circle and as she showed us the plastic fish that she brought with her, she told us to pass the fish around and to say one thing that we were thankful for today. I looked at her like she was crazy and thought, *Is she serious right now?* It made its way to several people, but by the time the fish got to one young man it was, pardon the pun, dead in the water. The young man held the fish, shook his head, and explicitly told the lady how ridiculous he thought the entire thing was. He then proceeded to turn that ugly looking clownfish into a flying fish as he hurled it over the couch where it landed on the nurse's desk, scattering the white papers on the table. Several of us giggled and the session was over. A few hours later they brought in another lady with a ukulele who offered to play us a few tunes of whatever we would like to hear. I went to my room and sat there for a minute and then I smiled for the first time in weeks thinking about how that plastic fish went flying across the room.

Suddenly, I was hit with a burst of emotions. It was like the Lord was showing me that there was a reason I was there seeing the things that I was seeing. The dam burst and the tears started to flow freely. I was broken. I was so broken for these people. I was broken for myself. I was broken for all the souls that I would never meet that go to psychiatric wards every day and don't get the help that they need. I was broken that the name of Jesus was never spoken once. I was broken that the best my state had to offer me was a plastic fish and a ukulele. I started to pray that the Lord would get me out of there as soon as possible. I promised Him that I would spend the rest of my life trying to heal my wounds so that I could also help bandage the wounds of others.

Forty-eight hours. I was there forty-eight long hours before the doctor finally decided to discharge me. I can't quite put into words the relief I felt walking out of that hospital. I felt like my chains had just been removed and I was walking out of my prison cell. I went back to my therapist and we started discussing my next steps and options. There were several inpatient facilities that I could have chosen, but the third option stood out to me the most. She said that there was a facility called Mercy Ministries that worked with young women ages twelve to thirty to deal with issues all the way from severe anxiety and depression to sex trafficking, and everything in between. I would get Christian counseling, room and board, and everything would be free of charge to me. It was an average six-month program, and they had multiple locations all over the country. I submitted my paperwork and a letter stating how much I would love the opportunity to participate in this program. They reviewed it and in one month they had placed me in St. Louis, Missouri. I was hoping to be placed in the Nashville location because that was only three hours away from my home and family. But little did I know what the Lord would teach me with that distance. The distance alone made the process so much harder and made me really think about how much I wanted freedom from these things that plagued me. I weighed out the options and decided that the distance was worth it. After my acceptance, they gave me two weeks to be in St. Louis. Those felt like the shortest two weeks of my life. I was ready for this big step but at the same time, I was terrified. I had never been away from my family that long and just the thought of being that far away from them scared me.

I arrived at Mercy Ministries, which is now known as Mercy Multiplied, on March 20, 2013, terrified but determined to let the Lord "fix" me and help me break away from the toxic patterns that I had now been practicing for twenty-one years. It was a huge, beautiful white house that could hold up to thirty girls at one time at full capacity. I was the southern belle of the bunch. The girls and ladies on staff always wanted me to pray before meals so they could hear me talk. I had only been there about a week when a huge snowstorm came through. It was one of the most gorgeous sights I had ever seen. A lot of girls from the northeast coast were there, so the snow wasn't a big deal for them. I remember sitting in a rocking chair on the huge porch at the house. I couldn't help but look out at the pure white snow. I had been playing in it earlier that day like a toddler, but now just sitting in the silence looking at the pure snow, it was untouched and without blemish. It was beautiful. It was breathtaking. It was a reminder to me that the color white could be a good thing.

Did you know the color white is mentioned in the Bible seventy-five times? Sometimes white can be a reminder from our Heavenly Father that He is truly a merciful God. As a matter of fact, in Lamentations it states that "His mercies are new every morning." A color that I had previously despised so much was now staring back at me in the purest form as an astounding reminder that I could still have a new, fresh start. The next six months were *full* of challenges. The first month was the hardest for me. I was only allowed to speak to my mom for fifteen minutes a day, twice on the weekends. That struggle in and of itself about killed me. I had to dig down deep and uncover old wounds that had scabbed over but had not properly healed. The staff at Mercy had to bandage me up like a little girl that had just fallen off her bike and scraped her knee. They had to wipe off the dirt, pour that awful hydrogen peroxide over the fresh wound, put some antibiotic ointment on it, and then bandage it up to ensure its proper healing to completion. Six months later I graduated from Mercy Ministries and felt like a new woman, ready to take on the world. I was ready to handle whatever Satan might throw my way.

Several months after graduation I started feeling very fatigued and thirsty all the time. I couldn't get enough to drink. I went to the doctor and they ran some blood work. One afternoon as I was on my way home from work, I got a call from my doctor's office. The nurse on the other end eloquently stated, "Hey . . . yeah . . . So, we ran bloodwork and it shows that you are a diabetic. Your sugar was over 400 today."

I felt sick. I didn't know what to say or how to respond. I felt the heat creep up the back of my neck and it just lingered there. Once the initial shock wore off, I cried. A lot. I cried out of frustration and fear, but I am ashamed to say that I think I mainly cried out of anger. I would tell God, "I could have ended it all, you know. I could have left this world or just simply made bad decisions, but I chose to leave my home for six months and get the help I thought You wanted me to get to improve my life!" I was so bitter. I did not in any way take care of myself the way I needed to. I would just let my sugar get sky high and eat whatever I wanted to because honestly, I was ticked. I was arrogantly living in denial and pretending that this vicious disease couldn't touch me. One year went by and I was misdiagnosed as a Type 2 diabetic. After a year, my sugar had not improved, and the medicine wouldn't touch my out of control glucose. I could drink Diet Coke and eat broccoli and my sugar would still be in the 200s. At the end of 2014, I was diagnosed as a Type 1 diabetic, which meant that my pancreas no longer produced insulin and that I would have to be on medication and an insulin pump for the rest of my life. That made me even angrier.

I was in a small group at church and one of the girls that was in the group came up to me after service was over. She stated that she had lived with Type 1 diabetes her entire life. She then proceeded to give me some perspective that would stick with me forever. She talked about how in the beginning everything was perfect. Adam and Eve had it made in paradise and then evil crept in and the world was forever changed by its touch. Disease is just part of the Fall and there is not a lot we can do about it. God isn't malicious. He loves his children. He doesn't get His kicks from seeing us suffer or bringing us pain. One day I was desperate for a word from the Lord, so I opened my Bible and just started flipping and scrolling. I was longing for God to speak to me. I flipped to John chapter 9, which tells a story of Jesus healing a blind man. After Jesus healed the blind man one of the disciples asked Jesus, "Rabbi, who sinned, this man or his parents, that he was born blind?"

"Neither this man nor his parents sinned," said Jesus, "but this happened so that the works of God might be displayed in him." That passage of Scripture hit me harder than a ton of bricks. It still gives me chills when I read it. I believe deep down in my soul that God was speaking to me through that passage, simply to say that He loves me. He hasn't forgotten about me nor forsaken me. I have this disease so that I can be used by Him in some way, shape, or form so that His works might be displayed through me. Admittedly, it is still hard, and some days I see the picture more clearly than others.

My last encounter with white would be on a very hot and humid day at the end of May. I remember standing in front of a full-length mirror staring at my reflection. For a moment I could have sworn that I saw that curly haired little girl with those two front teeth missing and a silly little grin. But I blinked, and there I was, now dressed head to toe in, you guessed it: white. All white. I was to be married on that day. I stood there having never felt more beautiful. I felt like everything had truly come full circle. The Lord was giving me the desire of my heart. He was giving me the man I had prayed for since I was a little girl. The next voice I heard was that of my daddy, gently asking if I was ready to start walking as he gave me his arm to hold on to. I could hear the swooshing of the tulle from my long train across that beautiful hardwood floor and my heart pounding in my ears. All I had to do now was look ahead of me and see my best friend standing at the end of the aisle, smiling through his tears. As I walked down that aisle, I saw an answered prayer. I saw my best friend, I saw the future father to my children, and I saw God's hand all over how we found each other.

My husband and I are both involved in full-time ministries. I get the honor of being given opportunities to try and shine a light on my past so that I can help others make better decisions and choices for their future and remind them that God has a purpose for their life. My life is more beautiful now than I ever dreamed it could be. I don't want to sound like Snow White prancing through the woods singing that life is perfect, but I can truly see God's favor on my life and evidence of how much He loves me. Not because of anything that I have accomplished, but simply because I'm His kid. It has been incredible to see what my life has become, and it makes my heart ache to think that it could have been cut short due to the evil thoughts Satan planted regarding my self-image in my young mind. So many things would have been left unexperienced, so many adventures left untaken, and so much love not felt. Let me remind you: YOU HAVE PURPOSE. God makes no mistakes even down to the number of hairs that rest upon your head. Don't ever let Satan, the enemy, cause you to believe otherwise.

CHAPTER 9

He Gives and Takes Away

The fluorescent light buzzed above my head as I nervously waited to see the outcome of the test lines that would determine my fate. A gas station bathroom wasn't exactly the atmosphere I had always pictured in my mind when receiving the news that I would have a baby. At this point, however, that didn't really matter. Whatever I may have imagined in my childhood dreams, the reality was that I was caught up in a current of unexpected circumstances. It was the summer before my senior year in high school, and my life wasn't anything like I had expected. The boy I was dating was six years older than me, a drug dealer, and notoriously "bad." And me? My life had spiraled down a path of alcohol, drugs, sex, and lies. There wasn't a faithful bone in my body as I abandoned God at the first sign of anyone who would give me the security I craved most.

I was raised as a "church girl" in a loving home, but affliction marked my life early on. My mom suffered with a brain tumor from my earliest memories, and my dad worked tirelessly to support and love us, truly exemplifying for me the sacrificial love of God, our Heavenly Father. Yet, my parents' marriage collapsed under the weight of years of conflict, and they divorced when I was twelve years old. This divorce was the catalyst for my mother's alcohol addiction. What time she wasn't in bed due to the brain tumor, she was unconscious because of alcoholism which became her other illness.

Looking back, I can see where my downward spiral started. I wasn't abused and I wasn't abandoned; I was simply alone, or at least that's how I felt. It was the loneliness I experienced at such a tender age that drove me to look for security and acceptance in various forms. I suffered from an insatiable need for affection and approval and anyone's attention would do. I had a hunger gnawing away at my soul—one that drugs, alcohol, or boys couldn't fill.

Unexpectedly, as I sat on the cold, dirty tile floor of the local gas station and saw two pink lines staring back at me, something inside of me sprang to life, something that had been cold and dormant for years. That something was called *hope*. I hoped that this baby would be my ticket out of the lonely world I had created, so I chose life because I knew that a new life offered hope. While it may not have happened exactly like I pictured, the new life growing inside me would be the very instrument God would use to give me new life through Jesus.

I had big dreams, some would even say big potential, but I had abandoned those dreams to grasp the phantom of affection. When my pregnancy was discovered I was told that my future was gone, that I had slept away my significance, and for a while I believed that lie. That is, until I held that tiny, perfect, newborn little boy in my arms and realized that God had given me another chance. Ironically, the very thing that people said would end my life, would instead be used as a vessel to save my life by the power of God. If I had never gotten pregnant and had continued down the path I was on, there's a chance I would not be alive today. Even through my recklessness, God relentlessly pursued me into a relationship with Him as He used my son to redirect my heart back to Jesus, the only One who could heal it.

Being raised as the "church girl" from a notable family, I was the scarlet letter written across my family tree. I carried a crushing weight of shame as I faced my parents, family, friends, and peers. But it wouldn't be the reaction of my family or my friends that scarred me the most. Instead, my biggest hurt would be the reaction from the church that I had attended all my life. These people were family to me. They were the same people who had graciously led me through my childhood and cared for me when my mother couldn't. Yes, they responded to my news by giving me the customary bridal and baby showers, just as they did for every new bride and mother-to-be. But instead of holding my showers within the church, it was held at the home of a church member because the holy sanctuary was not a "suitable" place. And while destination weddings were not yet a thing, I was also encouraged NOT to have my wedding inside the church because of my extenuating circumstances. To this day I believe the Lord stepped in and brought rain the week my outdoor wedding was planned, so that we did indeed get to have our ceremony in the sacred place of the church. Even though I was not rejected, I was restrained. Restrained from being in the very place I needed so desperately to be. Because of this reaction, I assumed that God wanted nothing to do with me, and that I was no longer welcome in His plan. My church family's response simply affirmed to me that my worst fear was true: I was no longer good enough for Jesus.

Through the ups and downs of teenage pregnancy and marriage, I was at the end of my rope. The lifestyle I wanted so desperately to escape followed me into my marriage. Neither of us knew how to live life any differently, and we didn't have the power within us to change. We cycled in and out of the same oppressive pits of alcohol and parties, when what we really needed was something bigger than ourselves. What we needed was the freedom of the cross. Not only was I crashing on a personal level, but my relationship with my husband also took a nosedive. As it turns out, partying with someone and being married to them are two extremely different things. We filed for divorce twice within the first year and a half of marriage, but somehow never followed through on taking the necessary steps to finalize it. By the grace of God, we are still married to this day. Two years and two babies into our marriage, I knew something had to change. Deep down within my soul I knew that I was meant for more than the unfulfilling life I was living. I knew I needed something bigger than myself to live for. I was empty with nothing to give to a child or my husband. I was unraveling at the seams and desperate for someone to save me from myself. Jeremiah 2:13 perfectly described my life: "a cracked cistern that could not hold water." So, I did what any church girl would do. I went to church.

On that night I barely had enough gas to make the drive from my house to the rural church I had once called home. I gathered quarters and pieced together stray change, hoping it would buy me a ride to my second chance. As I pulled into the parking lot, the darkness of night was nothing compared to the darkness of life's circumstances that weighed heavy on my soul. I carried my toddlers into the damp basement nursery and slid into the women's Bible study class. Being the youngest one by twenty years or more, I found my old sidekick, loneliness, creeping in. I was sure that I did not belong there. I don't know if it was the southern politeness ingrained in me or my own pride that kept me from leaving, but I decided to stay. The woman leading the class was different, and it seemed as if she knew a special secret that I didn't know. As the class began, I experienced something I had never experienced in any class before. I could sense in her a true fire for the Lord, and I could see the joy from her relationship with Him cascading out of her heart and into the room. In all my years of attending church I had never seen the Word of God like she saw it. Her love for the Lord was contagious, and I caught a full-blown case of it. She made me question my presumptions about the Lord, about His Word, and about His church. That night all the restrictions that once held me at bay came crashing down. When the dust settled, I felt God's grace, and I was changed forever.

I left that Bible study with fresh hope. I set my Bible in the passenger seat and as I headed home, I caught myself glancing over at it repeatedly. In that moment I realized that this was the book that held the secret the teacher seemed to know and that the answer to my longings could be found in that book as well. Once we were home and my babies were all safely tucked in bed,

I pulled the Bible to my chest and opened the pages to John 10 where my heart latched on to verse 10, "The thief comes only to steal and kill and destroy; I have come that they may have life, and have it to the full." *Fullness!* That was what I desperately wanted. My life up until that point had been anything but abundant. The promise of something more, something pure stirred in my heart. It was there in the pages of Scripture that I found what my soul had been longing for all along: Jesus. After years of searching, I had finally found the Savior who would heal my mind and give me a heart that was whole. Having lived for so long with the effects of the enemy and the torrent of destruction left behind, I gladly gave complete control of my life to the Lord. I was determined that from that moment on, I would never be the same.

At first my husband wasn't too sure about my newfound "obsession" with church and the Bible. He would bristle when anything spiritual was mentioned, even making fun of who I had become. Those were hard times, but eventually the contagious joy that I had caught that night in the women's study spread to him as well, and the Lord turned our lives completely around. I often tell people that if God saved our marriage, He could save any marriage, and I believe it to be true with all my heart. We are living proof that no relationship is so far gone that the cross of Christ cannot reach someone right where he or she is.

Psalm 119:71 states it perfectly: "It was good for me to suffer, so that I might learn your statutes" (NET). God used my suffering to draw me to Him, giving me everything when I had nothing to give in return. God gave me something precious amid my promiscuity. He gave my family redemption, saving us from the ruins of our lives. Now we had wholeness.

And the Lord takes away . . .

Years later, I would take another pregnancy test. This time it would take place in the comfort of my new home, with the security of my loving husband. Two unexpected lines once again appeared, also unplanned, but this time welcomed. We thought our nest was full, but God had other ideas. Having just purchased what we hoped would be our forever home, the timing was miraculous as the Lord provided a place for us to rest. I was so caught up in the process of moving that I didn't even notice the symptoms indicating pregnancy until I was around twelve weeks along.

The time came for the first doctor's visit, and we left the doctor's office with proof in hand of a healthy baby. I didn't know it at the time, but that black and white picture would be the first and last time I would hear that little heartbeat. We decided to wait about telling family until after the next doctor's visit, but one night after everyone had endured a long and trying week, we decided to lighten the mood by sharing our good news. Giving each of our children a bag containing a pacifier and an ultrasound picture, we instructed them to open it as we captured the sweet moment on video and sent it to our families. Everyone was thrilled.

I was unusually sick, and with this being my fourth pregnancy, I instinctively knew that something wasn't quite right. Doctors assured me that the severity of my symptoms was the result of living a fast-paced life as well as from being a little older. A month passed and my stomach grew, giving me comfort that growth was also happening on the inside and assurance that the doctors must surely be right. It's no surprise then that at my second doctor's visit when I was supposedly sixteen weeks along, I was alarmed as the nurse ran the cold probe of the handheld doppler machine over my protruding belly without finding the rhythm of a heartbeat. She assured me that the baby was probably just "hiding" and brought another nurse in to try, but to no avail. Several nurses ended up trying to coax our baby out of hiding, but when the fifth nurse couldn't find the rhythm of a heart, I knew the outcome was probably bleak. Their ultrasound machine was not working, so they ushered us into a neighboring practice's ultrasound room, where the deafening sound of a silent womb filled the tiny space. There in the same black and white frame we had looked at a month before was the motionless body of our baby with no heartbeat.

I often replay that moment in my mind as the picture of my baby's limp body remains frozen forever in a place in my heart. The doctor said our baby measured only twelve weeks, so I had been carrying his lifeless body for nearly a month. He must have passed shortly after my first visit, and the severe symptoms I experienced were my body's way of alerting me that something was wrong.

We left the doctor's office and drove to the school to pick up our children. Their smiling faces met us with questions about the baby and how our appointment had gone. I held back the tears as we made our way home and then sat down at the farmhouse table with my children and told them what had happened. The older kids, understanding what had been lost, wept and asked questions. They were hard questions including, "Why would God let this happen?"

The only answer I had was, "I don't know, but He is still good." I had never experienced pain as deep as the pain I felt in the wake that followed, nor have I experienced anything like it since. A year later I would also bury my mother, and as tragic and devastating as her death was, it didn't compare to the pain of losing my baby. I couldn't understand why God would take him. This pain I felt seemed unwarranted. I hadn't asked for another baby. I was content with the house full that I already had. Yet, one thing stands out above all else during that time: *God showed up.*

I also never experienced God's comfort and presence more than I did during that season of loss. He used affliction to show me His affection. One night, weeks later when the pain was suffocating, I remember asking God, "Why can't I get over this?" His reply that echoed through my spirit was, "You weren't meant to get over this. Some things in life we don't get over. Instead we are meant to use them as a platform to display God's goodness and glory."

The mountain of pain was the very mountain where I experienced the Lord transform me. I saw His glory there, despite the questions and the heartache. He showed up, and He stood me back on my feet.

One of the hardest things about having a miscarriage is that there is no tombstone, no death certificate, and no visible proof that the baby you carried and will always love was ever real. I learned through our experience that there are a million little choices we can make after such a loss to *choose life*. We choose life through every action we take to make sure that the brief life is remembered. For us, one of those choices was to give our baby a name. This simple act brought us so much healing. We also carry balloons to a Hope memorial statue in a local cemetery every year on the anniversary of the day we discovered his heart had stopped. Somehow giving him a name and honoring his life brings healing.

The story of David and the loss of his newborn son is what God used to comfort and heal me. In 2 Samuel 12:23, David, having just lost his baby stated during his sorrow, "I will go to him, but he will not return to me." Hope in heaven is what got David through and that is also what carried my family and me through. As David's story continued, he and Bathsheba would also have another son named Solomon, a son that the Lord loved (2 Samuel 13:24). Just like David, God has given to me and He has taken, but in the end God always redeems. Two months after our great loss, two pink lines appeared once more, and today we hold our own "Solomon." Redemption may not always be another baby, but there will always be an opportunity to arise from our ashes.

Through His grace there is purpose in our pain. One of the greatest promises we can hear is that our pain is not in vain and that we do not suffer without purpose. Suffering can be the greatest tool given for the sharing of the gospel, and sharing the gospel is the very reason why we are here. Lamentations 3:32 states, "Though he brings grief, he will show compassion, so great is his unfailing love."

I love that compassion follows grief. Grief is real but so is compassion. Our God is a God full of compassion and comfort. However, we must let Him comfort us as we put ourselves in a place of submission to His rule so that we can receive the peace of His touch. Don't be afraid to ask God questions. We may be perplexed but we are not in despair (2 Corinthians 4:9). He is good, even in the bad. He is gracious even when He takes.

Our view may not be clear, and we may not understand why we have suffered loss, but the fact that our hope is tethered not to our situation but to the throne, keeps us from despair. We are never stronger than when weakness is embraced because it is then that we are infused with the strength of Christ.

What I have learned through both the giving and the taking is that Christ is over all things and He is in all things. He owns all the pieces: all the broken areas of life, including the areas that aren't like we wanted or expected them to be. He owns all the areas that shout to us that we aren't enough, all the places where our understanding is clouded by the pain, and all the times that are stained by the stress of life. Every disappointment, every heartache, is fertile ground for the enemy to come and steal our purpose, our peace, and pleasure that God intends to give us. The enemy of our souls wants us to be so consumed with our scattered pieces that we never see the whole picture, or the purpose God has in mind for us. The enemy will play on our disappointments, tempting us to try to fix it ourselves, knowing all along that we can't fix things on our own. That is why we are empty as we try to control our chaos. There is only One who speaks and causes order to form out of chaos, and that is God. Just as He did at creation, He speaks into the void and creates life. He sends light where there was once darkness, and He causes chaos to bow to purpose. All these pieces we have don't make sense to us because we can't figure out how they all possibly join. We hold the pieces in our hands, thinking that they don't fit and that they don't belong in our puzzle. The truth is that it isn't the pieces that are the problem, but rather what we are building around them that causes the problem. To complete a complicated puzzle, we must first see the picture of how it is intended to look. Without the picture to refer to, the scattered individual pieces simply form chaos. There is no order because there is no image. "The Son is the image of the invisible God, the firstborn over all creation" (Colossians 1:15).

The same thing happens with all the pieces of our lives. All the disappointments as well as all the joys are to form a complete picture of His plan for our lives. Unless we keep our eye on the Image, we lose sight of how all of this is supposed to be. Our lives are to replicate God. Just as a puzzle makes the image on the box come to life, we as Christ followers are being made into His likeness, piece by piece, to show the world His fullness. Things only make sense when Christ is at the center. We are called to a full life, a life that replicates the image of God. We are told in Colossians 2:9-10 that all the fullness of Christ has been given to us. An important concept we must grasp is that emptiness is a prerequisite for fullness. Only when we are empty are we ready to be filled! To live in fullness, we must first understand that when *ALL* the pieces of our lives center around Christ, they will show a picture of what fullness really looks like.

"Fullness" in the Greek language is *pleroo*, which means "to make complete in every particular, to cause to abound, to furnish and supple, to flood, to diffuse throughout, to pervade, to take possession of and so to have ultimate control."[2] That is what we are looking for! We are all, every person on this planet, seeking to be complete. *Every. Single. One.* You see, to be filled requires ownership. For something or someone to fill something they must have possession of that object, as well as complete rule and authority. Fullness comes when we give Christ complete control of our lives, which includes the good and the bad.

> "The Son is the image of the invisible God, the firstborn over all creation. For in him all things were created: things in heaven and on earth, visible and invisible, whether thrones or powers or rulers or authorities; all things have been created through him and for him. He is before all things, and in him all things hold together. And he is the head of the body, the church; he

---

2 Spiros Zodhiates, ed. *The Complete Word Study Dictionary* (United States: AMG Publishers, 1992), 1177.

is the beginning and the firstborn from among the dead, so that in everything he might have the supremacy. For God was pleased to have all his fullness dwell in him, and through him to reconcile to himself all things, whether things on earth or things in heaven, by making peace through his blood, shed on the cross" (Colossians 1:15-20).

These verses healed my broken heart. They gave me comfort that nothing else in this world could. They tell us of Christ's supremacy, or as scholars say, His preeminence: Christ's right to rule. In these verses Paul tells us that the key to our fullness lies in the supremacy of Christ. Understanding that all things are His will can lead to our growth if we cooperate and embrace it.

We are told another important fact in Colossians 2:14-15: "having canceled the charge of our legal indebtedness, which stood against us and condemned us; he has taken it away, nailing it to the cross. And having disarmed the powers and authorities, he made a public spectacle of them, triumphing over them on the cross." This verse was a vital tool that God gave me to walk in fullness. It means that Christ took away everything that the enemy had on me and may possibly have on you. It means that as the nails drove into His hands, it was as if our sin, shame, and betrayal, all hung there with Him as He bled and died for us. Our past sins are dead, and it is important that we fully understand that, just as I had to do to move into the abundant life that He had for me. Christ has taken the authority of shame away so that it cannot hold us any longer—shame has no right. Christ has delivered us from every power that would try and claim the title of our purpose. Hear this loud and clear, and let it sink deeply into your heart: the way you live your life is meant to heap shame *on the enemy's head*. Once I realized that, I lived differently. The very shame the devil has plotted to use to take us down is the same shame that will be his disgrace. Christ wants to turn the very thing that Satan has plotted to use against us into our means for victory over him. When we choose to live a crucified life, fully submitted to Christ in all things, then we make a fool out of the enemy.

There is a battle for our loyalty and who or what we will allow our hearts to be ruled by. Satan doesn't tempt many of us to worship him because he knows we won't. That's way too obvious, so he uses a different approach called "deception." Satan masquerades as an angel of light, getting us to hand the throne of our hearts to anyone and anything other than Christ. Christ is meant to rule all things, and half-hearted obedience should never be a part of the equation. We must choose to give Him the pieces of our lives so that we can experience the fullness of His. "All things" mean nothing is out of Christ's reach, and nothing is beyond His control. He is the guardian over all our pieces. "All things" mean that nothing is exempt from His care—*nothing*. That means our success cannot rise beyond His victory. Nothing is outside Christ's sphere of influence. Every single piece of our lives and every molecule of creation, seen and unseen, is contained by Christ. Nothing gets out of His control. He is the reference point for all things. That means that tragedy and triumph must be on Christ's terms; He is the boundary line, and nothing can break out of His borders. All things are in His jurisdiction.

One of the greatest threats I faced during my time of loss was that of my heart growing hard against God. Whenever we face trials, we are at risk of becoming callous as our hearts grow weather-worn from the storms. We can become captive to disappointment and expect always to be let down. A telltale sign of a hard heart is the expectation of disappointment. Dread is nothing more than expectation that has been hijacked by fear. We grow afraid instead of expectant. But that's not the life we are called to live. Psalm 112:7 says, "They will have no fear of bad news; their hearts are steadfast, trusting in the Lord." I do know that if we give in to disappointment, we can become captives to it, and it can taint the way we see everything. As a result, we may see God as a taker instead of as a giver. When this becomes our perception, we will not be able to enjoy what God is doing because we are suspicious that it will all end badly. I know this because it happened to me. Disappointment causes us to see God's gracious intervention in our lives as coincidence, but the things that are working *for* us are not coincidence but Christ! Chronic disappointment wants us to retreat. In the season of loss that I experienced, I was expecting defeat, and let me assure you that mindset is no way to live. We must reorient our expectations to experience freedom.

We live in a fallen world, where things are broken and the sharp shards of fallenness can cut deep. But when we understand that all these pieces are in Christ's jurisdiction, then we live differently. Brokenness no longer defines us, but instead, Christ does. Because all things are in Him, it means that all things are subject to His redeeming touch. There is purpose in the pieces because as Romans 8:28 says, "And we know that in all things God works for the good of those who love Him . . . " Because all things which include all of your pieces are "in Christ," that means that no matter how tragic or harsh the circumstance is, Christ owns it, and He *will* use it to shame the enemy, to bring us wholeness, and to bring glory to Himself. He is for us, and because He is for us, all things work for our ultimate good and His glory. It may not always work to our comfort or work out our way, but we can know it will always be for our good. The trap we often fall into is to set our mind on thinking that it is either one or the other: God's glory or our good. If we separate God's glory from our good, we will always expect disappointment. God's glory never disappoints because it always works for our good. His glory is not selfish, but rather works for us *and* for Him, to bring us to fullness. All things must work out for our good and they have no other option because we are in Christ and Christ is in us. That's the hope that supremacy brought me through loss and through gain. As I have experienced both the giving and the taking, I can honestly say, *Blessed be the name of the Lord for He is good,* even in grief. We can trust Him in all things.

CHAPTER 10

Moments That Define Us

Have you ever thought about those events in your life that fundamentally changed you from who you thought you were going to be to who you actually became? You'll often hear these events referred to as *defining moments* in life. A defining moment could literally be anything that occurred at any moment in your life. It might have been a pivotal decision that altered the direction of your life. Maybe it was the moment that you or a loved one received an unexpected medical diagnosis. Perhaps it was the moment that your future spouse asked you for that first date. Or maybe it was the job you decided to take or finally gathered enough courage to leave. A defining moment might *even* have occurred without us realizing it at the time. In hindsight, I now know that one of my life's most defining moments, aside from my salvation, occurred three years before I was aware that it had taken place.

While I was involved in a ladies' Bible study entitled *He Speaks to Me* by Priscilla Shirer,[3] God revealed things to me about my journey as the mother of a special needs' son. On this night, we watched a video of Priscilla teaching about being still to listen to God. One of the Scriptures that she used in her lesson was from Job 33:14-16: while we sleep, He (God) "opens the ears of men and seals their instruction" (AMP). As we went through the study guide, God reminded me that He had already spoken to me about this major life situation

---

3   "He speaks To Me: Preparing To Hear From God," Session 4 Video Teaching Session, Priscilla Shirer

before my third child was even born. Immediately my thoughts turned back to a night when I was pregnant with my son. I recalled waking abruptly from my sleep with my heart pounding. Surely God had not just spoken to me in the middle of the night. But He had. He spoke to me about the child I was carrying. I heard Him say, "Everything with this baby is not all right. Your life is going to be changed because of this, but everything will be okay."

I didn't understand what was going on. I was accustomed to the labor experiences I had when delivering my daughters, both born at thirty-seven weeks with no issues. Maybe that's why I dismissed this experience and never told anyone about being awakened in the night with this news. After all, this pregnancy had come as somewhat of a happy surprise, and I was ashamed that any negative thoughts like this even came to my mind.

Until hearing this Scripture, I didn't realize that God had spoken peace and comfort to my heart the night He woke me up. At the time I didn't interpret His words as peaceful or encouraging even though He had said it was going to be "okay." (I know you must be thinking that God surely didn't use the slang "okay," but that is all I have ever been able to remember from that night.) He must have been patiently waiting for me to discover this truth in His Word so that His Spirit could now reveal to me that He had truly spoken to my heart that night in the summer of 2005.

It was in the spring of 2002 that my husband and I were surprised to learn that we were expecting our son. The pregnancy seemed routine, but early on my doctor told me that she wanted to do an ultrasound when I was around seven months along because I had experienced early contractions with my two girls. The result of the ultrasound revealed the first hint that everything might not be business as usual this time around. I remember driving home from the doctor's office on a November afternoon knowing we would soon be going to Birmingham for a "targeted" ultrasound. After two different ultrasounds at our regular doctor's office, we were getting conflicting reports of "a polycystic kidney" and "an absent kidney." I remember exactly where we were in our journey when I told my husband how scared I was. I told him I realized that as Christians we are told to expect that we will experience storms in our lives and that since things had been going smoothly for us, it could very well be time for us to encounter such a storm. Looking back to that moment, I certainly did not expect that the storm would come through the birth of our son and change the course of our lives forever.

We were so relieved when the "targeted" ultrasound showed that everything was normal regarding our baby's kidneys. Around thirty-seven weeks, my water broke and less than twelve hours later, our son was born. I was totally caught off guard when the doctors and nurses told me he weighed only 4 lbs and 8 oz. Even though his lungs functioned well, our son's color wasn't good for a newborn, and he was very weak. I can still remember how pitiful he looked when he cried. He was so thin that his little face didn't have any baby fat. While we were trying to overcome the shock, I was immediately questioned by hospital staff. *Had I smoked during my pregnancy or taken drugs?* They asked many other questions about things that might have affected his growth. This upset me terribly since I knew I had done nothing of the sort. Because he was so weak, our son was unable to nurse or even take a bottle. So, I began pumping milk for him. We were finally able to get him to take the milk through a very small tube that we would tape to a finger and touch to the roof of his mouth as we tried to stimulate his sucking reflex. It was a very slow process, but we were thrilled just to be able to get some nourishment into his tiny little body. He also became jaundiced and had to spend the time that he was not being fed resting under the special light in the nursery in hopes of getting his bilirubin number to a normal range. Nothing was ever critical, but things just certainly were not as they should be. I guess, thinking back to that night God spoke to my heart, that everything really was "okay" like He said it would be.

Our son never had to be in the neonatal care unit, and we were able to keep him in the room with us quite a bit. I remember rolling him in his little bassinet into the nursery at 2 a.m. each morning to be weighed and to have his blood tested. This actually became the highlight of our day since the goal during this time was for him to gain weight and get his bilirubin to a normal level so that we could take him home to our girls and begin to live as a family of five. I think God even allowed us to find a bit of humor to sustain us during this time. I remember telling my husband that I felt like we were taking our fish to be weighed at a fishing tournament each morning as we reported for our son's big "weigh in."

After ten long days in the hospital, he gained just enough weight that the doctor felt that he was moving in the right direction, and we were finally able to bring our baby home. It was so good to get home to my sweet girls. Our oldest girl was five, and the youngest just two-and-a-half years old. Oh, how they loved their baby brother, and from the very beginning they were smitten by him! To this day he knows they are his biggest fans, and that they will do almost anything to make him happy. That might mean singing and dancing to Disney songs with him, taking him to McDonald's or Cracker Barrel, or acting out his favorite game show, "Deal or No Deal."

While we were in the hospital a very well-meaning nurse told me that she thought I would be a great mother to a special needs child. She told me that she thought I "had what it takes." Mind you, this was probably within twenty-four hours of my son being born. While she didn't mean anything unkind by her comment, I know now that I was not yet ready to hear that. At that point, no one had really said anything quite that blunt to me about my son's condition. I think that in those very early days of his life, I was so blindsided by our family's new reality that at times, I thought I would wake up and find that everything about my son would be *normal*. However, even though I had all these different emotions and questions, I always had peace, a peace that I really didn't understand, and a comfort that could not be explained. Throughout my life I had read Philippians 4:7, which says, "And the peace of God, which transcends all understanding, will guard your hearts and your minds in Christ Jesus." I had often wondered what that kind of peace would look or feel like. The word *transcends* means "to go beyond the range or limits of." That kind of peace, a peace that is "totally off the charts," will guard our hearts and minds.

As I was living through circumstances that I know I could not have handled on my own, it was God who was holding this mama's heart in His hands and giving me clarity of thought to do what I had to do each day to take care of my baby boy, but also to care for my daughters who were still little girls. I cannot begin to tell you how awestruck I was by God's goodness, mercy, and grace in the most difficult season of my life. There is absolutely no other explanation than to say that God truly sustained me. It was during these days that I began to see that God was going to use every minute detail of my son's journey to remind me that He really did have his life in His hands and that He really did have a plan for this child. God really did know my son when He put him together inside of my womb. I realized that it wasn't about me trying to figure out what was "wrong" with my baby or what could have happened while he was in utero. It was about me trusting God daily to take care of my precious boy right where he was and just as he was.

Is that not how God loves us? Doesn't He love us right where we are no matter what our circumstances are? It was God who had entrusted my husband and me to care for this child. I could tell story after story about how God has worked out so many issues with our son for His glory and our son's good. I have many stories about doctors who have prayed for our son, stories where God intervened and moved us from one doctor to another and often into better hands. Our stories were never as bad as it seemed because God was always one step ahead of us working all things for our good. As the years have gone by, I have learned to lean in and listen and be aware of God moving in these types of situations. I have learned that when I listen to God about something it gets easier to discern His voice the next time and not doubt that He really is the One speaking into a situation.

Remember we thought our son didn't have any kidney problems? When he was almost a year old, we discovered that he actually did have an absent kidney. My first instinct was to be upset about the incorrect diagnosis we had previously received. But God immediately spoke to my heart and told me that I really had not needed to know about this issue before my baby was born. He knew that at that point in life my faith was not yet mature enough to handle the knowledge that my son only had one kidney. God has always been faithful to give us just what we needed at just the right time for each season of our son's life. When he was two years old, it was time to take him back to the doctors to check his kidney again. The results were that the one kidney had grown to compensate for the absent kidney. We didn't need to see a specialist and we were thrilled with this news. That missing kidney? Turns out it was just one less thing for us to worry about!

Our son has never had any life-threatening health issues. However, in addition to delays in speech, growth, motor skills, and intellectual development, we later discovered that he had mild to moderate hearing loss, a submucous cleft palate, some degree of scoliosis, and a minor seizure disorder called "absence seizures" which appear more like long blinks, but actually show up as seizure activity on an EEG. When I read back through this list, I am reminded of how God took these problems and replaced my fears with faith in each circumstance.

It's obvious that God has used and will continue to use my son's life to teach lessons of faith to our family, all while bringing glory to Himself. I don't claim to be the perfect mom (especially in the sense of being a special needs' mom), some type of expert, or even to have the answers to many of the questions I face daily. I get distracted, overwhelmed, anxious, and worried. I could have chosen hopelessness on so many occasions, but instead the One in whom all my hope is found has faithfully reminded me that He has a perfect plan and purpose for these situations and for my child's life. I have read many times in Jeremiah 29:11 that "He knows the plans He has for us and that His plans are to prosper us and not to harm us, plans to give us a future and a hope." That promise is for us all! I choose to claim that promise for this child of mine.

We have always been amazed at how many people know our son and how many friends he has. If I am ever at school with him, kids of all ages will wave and call out "Hi, _____!" When we go to the grocery store near our home, the cashiers know our son by name. They also know that he is certain to buy a package of macaroni salad from the deli! My husband still talks about the first time he took our son to the high school football game and how it seemed that he knew everyone at the school and in the community. My husband said he didn't think he was going to get our boy out of the stadium because he got stopped by so many people that knew him. We have been at cross country meets where he would slip away from us to make friends with runners from other teams. Several weeks ago, we were in a shoe store in a nearby city and after finding him some shoes, I went to look at the ladies' shoes for just a minute. By the time I had gone down one aisle, he was leading three employees (all young ladies, of course) around the store in what appeared to be a game of follow the leader.

Our son easily makes friends, and God has also gifted him with a very caring spirit. He always wants to give hugs at church. It's not unusual for people to tell me that he gives the "best hugs." Not only does he want to give hugs to family members when he is saying good-bye, but he makes sure that his dad, sisters, and I also give hugs. He also wants everyone around him to get along. If he thinks someone is raising his or her voice or if his dad and I are in "an intense moment of fellowship" as our pastor calls it, he will come to where we are, and tell us to tell each other we are sorry. Talk about conviction from the mouths of babes!

One would not expect a child like this to read emotions very well, but he always seems to notice if someone is sad or hurting. Probably the most profound example of his sweet, caring spirit would be when he was almost twelve years old at his grandmother's funeral. I have often wondered what he understood about that day. Did he realize that his grandmother wouldn't be here for him anymore, or that she would not be at Papa's house when he went to visit the next time? He stood in the receiving line with us the entire time. The preacher made a point in his message to comment about how our son was there to give hugs and just love on everyone because he knew something was wrong, and he did what he knew to do to help. He might not have really understood what was going on, but he was doing exactly what his grandmother would have wanted him to be doing. He was caring for others and trying to make them feel better with his hugs. Despite my concerns about his understanding of the situation, he was using the personality and traits God had given him to bless and comfort others just by being himself.

Having a special needs child is certainly not always easy. Probably the biggest issue that we have dealt with throughout the years is that our son doesn't always transition from one activity to another easily. Often this causes what seems to be an unnecessary lack of cooperation. This brings a great deal of stress to family outings. Sometimes just getting into the car and riding to church can be such an unpleasant experience that it would be easy to just give up and go back home. We have never done that; we go to church each week because that is what we do. We have learned throughout the years that if we give him a few minutes to gain his bearings, he will soon settle down. It's not that he doesn't want to go to church; he just doesn't want to leave home. He really loves church and his church family. And thankfully his church family loves him.

Many times, I have felt so bad for my daughters, and not because they have a brother with special needs. It's because it's sometimes hard to go places and do even the simple things that should be enjoyable for us all. However, more times than not, we work through my son's issues before we get to the "fun." But I have never ceased to be amazed at the patience and character that my daughters have gained through the life experiences they have had living with a special needs brother. They have learned so much about selflessness and kindness by spending time doing the things their brother likes to do, and he adores them as well. I've often heard that if you want to know how to treat a special needs child, just watch the *siblings* of a special needs child. With all my heart I believe this to be true. Because my daughters know how to treat a special needs child, I have often seen them reach out to other special needs children and families we have met throughout the years.

From the time our son was very young, he has had speech therapy, physical therapy, and occupational therapy. His sisters have both participated and at different times gone with me to carry him for treatment. They have also worked to help me reinforce at home what was worked on in his therapy sessions. For my older daughter, her brother's treatment made such an impact that she has chosen to pursue occupational therapy for a career, and she is currently enrolled in a graduate program to earn her master's degree in Occupational Therapy. She truly feels like her experiences with her brother have guided her to choose this field so that she can help others gain improved skills that will add value to the quality of their lives.

Not only have I seen my son bring out the best in his sisters, but I have also noticed that he brings out the best in those around him. When he was in the sixth grade, my friend and I volunteered to use our family's race timing equipment to time the students in the physical education classes as they ran one mile. They had been training as part of the Presidential Fitness program at school, and this was the day that they would run to get their best time. My son had completed several one-mile races. We discovered that running one mile wasn't too hard for him if he ran at his own speed, which is quite a bit slower than most sixth grade boys. The course for the class run ended on a track that goes around the school's football field with the last quarter mile of the race taking place on the track itself. Most of the boys had already completed their runs, when my son finally got back into the stadium to begin the final lap that would bring him to the finish line.

A group of the boys was sitting on the grass near me, and as my son ran onto the track, I heard one of them say, "There he comes!" and all of them, probably six or seven boys, jumped up and ran to him and began running beside and behind him. They ran with him all the way around the track and as he was running that last hundred-yard stretch to the finish line, the young men cheered for him to finish strong, calling out his name and saying, "Go! You can do it!"

I grabbed my phone to capture the moment. I was so proud of my son and those boys, the kind of pride that brings tears to your eyes. Not only was my child a winner because he crossed the finish line, he was a winner because he had the support of this group of boys. These boys were also winners in my eyes because of their genuine attitudes and enthusiasm for their friend's big accomplishment. Once again, my son was using the personality and traits God had given him to bring out the best in others just by being who God created him to be.

Our son is now seventeen years old, and there won't be many more years that he will be able to attend his safe zone of public school. As the end of that time is approaching, his dad and I are starting to consider what will be next for him. I have to say that this is quite a scary time in our lives with so much uncertainty ahead. Will he be able to get some type of job? Will there be some type of day program that will meet his needs and allow him to reach his full potential? I often imagine him having a job at our local grocery store or possibly clearing tables at a restaurant. Or, will he work with my husband at our running shoe store after my husband retires from his "real" job?

To be honest, thinking about our son's future can be overwhelming for many reasons. It's in those moments of fear that I must choose to remember what God has already done in his life. God has always prepared the way and has continually worked out circumstances for His glory and our family's good. In 1 Samuel chapter 7, we read how Samuel commemorated God's help in battle by setting a stone he called "Ebenezer" and saying, "Thus far the Lord has helped us." It's at this point in my son's journey that it's important for me to look at the *Ebenezers* in our lives. I know at those times God helped, protected, and provided for my precious child and our family. Looking back at what I know, God gives me assurance that I can look forward to how He is going to work things out in the future. It would be all too easy to crouch in fear, but I am choosing instead to cling to the words that Paul wrote to young Timothy. "For the Spirit God gave us does not make us timid, but gives us power, love and self-discipline" (2 Timothy 1:7). I have learned to recognize that any fear that I feel is not from God. I am continually learning to replace those fears with faith. I must daily remember that "faith is confidence in what we hope for and assurance about what we do not see." (Hebrews 11:1) as I lean on the acronym that I learned for faith when I was younger: "Forsaking All I Trust In Him."

Thinking back to that defining moment when God spoke to me in the night so long ago . . . did God *really* tell me that everything would be okay? Did he really use the word "okay" with him being God and all? Of course, He did. He knew that was going to be one of my son's favorite words: "OKAY." 'Okay, okay, okay," he'll say. "Are you okay, Mama? It's okay."

Of course, it's okay, son. God knew it would be that way. Even before you were born.

Conclusion

Philippians 1:12-14 states, "Now I want you to know, brothers and sisters, that what has happened to me has actually served to advance the gospel. As a result, it has become clear throughout the whole palace guard and to everyone else that I am in chains for Christ. And because of my chains, most of the brothers and sisters have become confident in the Lord and dare all the more to proclaim the gospel without fear."

This one passage truly summarizes the stories presented in this book and ties them all together like a big, beautiful bow wrapped around the amazing gift of raw honesty that you've read in these pages. Not one of the ladies who signed up to write her story hopes to become famous. Not one of them received any payment for their work, nor did they know if this book would ever be published. They simply agreed to share their stories with the hope of helping someone just like you. They shared because they like Paul, the disciple who penned the above verse even while in chains, wanted you to see that what has happened to *you* can *also* serve to advance the gospel of Christ. They wrote their stories to provide a reason for you, in the chains of your suffering, to become more confident in the Lord and to speak more boldly for Him without fear or worry of what others might think! Their hearts' desires are for you to know Him.

Let me ask a very personal question. Do you know Christ as your Savior, and have you dedicated your life to living in daily relationship with Him? If so, then you can confidently call yourself a child of God and begin today to enjoy living in the peace that He gives. However, if you haven't prayed to accept Christ as your Savior, I would ask that you please not wait one moment longer to accept the gift of salvation that is freely available to you through Him. You can simply pray right where you are to accept the sacrifice that Jesus made on the cross as payment in full for your sins—past, present, and future. His sacrifice is the only thing that makes any of us righteous in the sight of God. Once you've prayed that prayer, you can begin to enjoy a personal relationship with God through Christ right now! And by "that prayer," I'm simply referring to a prayer composed of any words that you might choose to use to admit that you are a sinner in need of a Savior, who desires to give your life to God. Humble your heart and make a sincere profession of faith in Christ as the Lord of your life and the Savior of your soul. I personally like this very simple six-word prayer often offered by Erwin McManus at the end of his sermons: *God I give You my life*. It really is that easy. Such simple words, but such big meaning!

After praying for salvation, do not wait to go to Heaven to know Christ more. Begin conversing with Him today. Read His Word to hear how He will respond. Attend a Bible believing church to hear sermons, engage in life groups or studies, and various other activities that will encourage growth and renewal from the inside out . . . It is here that you will meet individuals who will mentor and support you through friendship and personal relationships as you face the obstacles and challenges of daily life.

I have no doubt that God desires a relationship with all of us that is beyond our wildest dreams, and one that will be more real to us than any human relationship that we have ever experienced! I hope that you will dare to take Him up on His offer of salvation . . . starting right now. What are you waiting for? If you mean it, pray it and watch your life change: *God, I give you my life*.

Questions for Group Discussion or Personal Reflection

Chapter 1: A Child of Addiction

"I will be a Father to you, and you will be my sons and daughters, says the Lord Almighty." 2 Corinthians 6:18

1. We often wonder how two people can commit the same sin and yet one walks away and the other pays a heavy price. The writer of this chapter saw the mercy of God displayed toward her stepdad as he made a conscious choice to turn from his addiction and choose a different path. People often think that they can continue to revisit unhealthy ways or actions if they don't do it "full time." It's easy to see how that would not be a wise choice for a drug addict, but what about other types of unhealthy choices?

2. The one that turned from his addiction in this story is now being used to help others turn and find healing from their addictions as well. His sin didn't disqualify him from being used in service to God. Have you ever felt disqualified from serving God in some way because of choices you made in the past? How do you feel about that now?

3. People often abuse prescription drugs. Because the word *prescription* is attached and the drug is administered by a pharmacy instead of a

drug lord, it's as if the addiction factor is nullified. 1 Corinthians 6:12 says, "'I have the right to do anything,' you say—but not everything is beneficial. 'I have the right to do anything'—but I will not be mastered by anything." If you think that you or someone you know is misusing or is addicted to prescription drugs, or perhaps is struggling with alcohol abuse, Google search "signs of drug/alcohol addiction." If you recognize any of the symptoms listed, acknowledge the addiction and address it now.[4]

4. My friend allowed her life experiences to help guide her to a career path that enables her to minister to others from the hurt that she endured. Often your greatest ministry will come from your greatest pain. Whatever you are walking through now or may have walked through in the past, rest assured that God can and will use it for your good and His glory if you will allow Him. Can you think of a way that He might possibly use your hardship or experience in a positive way?

5. The writer acknowledges her longing for a father in her life. If your father was absent in your life, know that you can still have a father. God Himself wants to be your father! My friend admitted that she tried to find comfort in relationships with other males to fill the void left by her father. Maybe you use relationships, or material items, food, or other things to fill an emptiness in your own life. There is a place in your heart that will never be satisfied by anything but Christ. If you are looking for love in all the wrong places, whether that be through drugs, bars, men, shopping, food, or anything else, it is not too late to stop. True to His Father's heart, He loves you no matter what you have done or where you have been. To learn more about how to experience His love for you, refer to the last chapter of this book.

---

4   https://www.drugabuse.gov/publications/research-reports/misuse-prescription-drugs/what-scope-prescription-drug-misuse

Chapter 2: Abortion and Depression

"I will exalt you, my God the King; I will praise your name for ever and ever. Every day I will praise your name for ever and ever. Great is the LORD and most worthy of praise; his greatness no one can fathom." Psalm 145:1-3

1. Do you feel that you, like the writer, have learned to count it all joy when you face difficult circumstances? Give some examples of ways that you have grown as a result of difficulties you have faced.

2. Would you say that your Christian walk has been a persistent path of progress toward sanctification? If not, why?

3. How do you handle confrontation? Remember that when possible, allowing time to process a situation before confronting someone can be very helpful in choosing the right words to say and in developing a positive approach that will resolve the issue. Proverbs 15:1 is a great verse to keep in mind when dealing with confrontation: "A gentle answer turns away wrath, but a harsh word stirs up anger." The more you practice addressing issues, the better you will become at it.

4. How much value do you place on the spiritual state of people with whom you are deeply involved? Whether in business, in dating, in advising, etc., it is important that you choose like-minded people when putting down "roots." In 2 Corinthians 6:14 we are told not to be unequally yoked with unbelievers. The Message translation states it this way: "Don't become partners with those who reject God. How can you make a partnership out of right and wrong? That's not partnership; that's war. Is light best friends with dark? Does Christ go strolling with the Devil? Do trust and mistrust hold hands? Who would think of setting up pagan idols in God's holy Temple? But that is exactly what we are, each of us a temple in whom God lives. God put it this way: 'I'll live in them, move into them; I'll be their God and

they'll be my people. So leave the corruption and compromise; leave it for good,' says God. 'Don't link up with those who will pollute you. I want you all for myself. I'll be a Father to you; you'll be sons and daughters to me.' The Word of the Master, God."

5. Are there decisions that you made recently or even years ago that still haunt you? It is important that you acknowledge your life choices for what they truly are and take them to God. Like the writer, many of us struggle with calling a sin by its true name. For example, it's much easier to say that we "stretched the truth" than it is to admit that we just told a big fat lie. Peace only comes when we acknowledge our sin to God and follow His path for healing. Is there anything that you need to acknowledge as sin before God today?

6. Is God the ruler of your life? If you answered no, then why not? What will it take for you to hand over the throne of your heart to Him? Tell Him what holds you back from trusting Him and then pray the verse at the top of this page each day, exalting God as the King who is worthy of your praise, who is greater than any you could ever imagine, and who is trustworthy to rule your heart.

Chapter 3: Infertility Issues

"For I know the plans I have for you,' declares the LORD, 'plans to prosper you and not to harm you, plans to give you hope and a future. Then you will call on me and come and pray to me and I will listen to you.'" Jeremiah 29:11

1. Everybody has a dream and plan in mind for the course their life will take. But sometimes things don't turn out quite like we planned. Do you have a dream that remains unfulfilled? If so, what is it? Maybe you've never even had the courage to voice your dream before, but it just might be time to do so now. Even though this writer didn't see her dream immediately come to pass, she didn't stop asking or

seeking God for the answer she desired. You shouldn't either. Now might be a good time to read through Luke 18:1-8, where God tells a parable about a woman who is rewarded for her persistence. Rest assured that He will answer your prayers, too: either by giving you your heart's desire or by giving you what He knows to be best for you. But either way, He will answer because He hears every prayer we ever pray.

2. Have you ever endured a season of suffering, whether physical or emotional, and felt like no one understood or even acknowledged your pain? Scripture tells us to mourn with those who mourn (Romans 12:15) and to carry one another's burdens (Galatians 6:2). One of our greatest opportunities to share the love of Christ with this world is when we minister to someone who is in need. Look around you today to see if you can identify someone within your sphere of influence who needs a friend or someone to help shoulder their load. It may be that God has given you an awesome opportunity to sow seeds of hope into their life by ministering to them in their trying circumstance.

3. Infertility is something that many couples struggle with. If you have endured this struggle you probably understand well the things people say that can be so insensitive. If you or your marriage have suffered with this issue, let me encourage you to know that you are not alone, and that God can still fill your life, your home, and your marriage with fullness and joy. Ask Him to reveal His plan to you and then trust His faithfulness and His plans which are always meant to prosper you and never to harm you. Make a list of ways you can continue to nurture other aspects of your marriage as you allow God's unique plan for your home to unfold.

4. I love how the writer answered the call from the hospital, spoke with the lawyer, took her requests to the Lord in prayer, and then went

back to fulfilling the responsibilities of her daily tasks. She didn't sit wringing her hands and pacing the floor, and she didn't spend her time worrying or chasing people down to ask for their opinions. She simply did what she could do, prayed an intimate prayer to the Lord, and then went back to her work. What a wonderful example of faith to those around her! Is there anything in your own life that is out of your hands and beyond your control? Take it to God in prayer and then leave it with Him. Don't waste your time trying to manipulate or maneuver things to go your way. Just pray and trust Him and then go about the things that you know you are responsible for doing. God is full of surprises and we must never forget it. When it feels like we've come to the end of our rope, we should remember that He is the God of all hope. Memorize Romans 15:13 and allow it to come alive in you by the power of the Holy Spirit.

5. In watching the impact of this writer's faithful relationship with the Lord through the good and the bad, I have observed how her story has allowed people to see God's hand at work in an undeniable way. I am certain that because of her journey there are people who know Christ as their Lord and Savior that otherwise would not. I will never forget the day that she received the phone call about her baby boy and how her experience impacted my heart even though it didn't change anything about my life circumstances. Years later as I drove by their house on the way to my home and saw him outside playing in the dirt with his trucks, I continued to thank God for His intervention and His faithfulness in our lives. Even now, as our daughters regularly play sports together and have sleepovers with friends, I thank Him for the work He has done in creating their family. If her story touched your heart as well, and if you, too, want to believe Him for things you could never imagine, turn to the last chapter of this book now to hear how He wants to pour out His love and joy in your life, too.

Chapter 4: Infidelity and Abortion
"And God will wipe away every tear from their eyes." Revelation 7:17

1. Most of us have things that we believe and values that we stand firmly on, until we face an unfortunate situation. Have you ever compromised your core beliefs or standards when you came face to face with a personal challenge? What were the results?

2. Any time we try to fill a void in our lives with a person or a thing instead of God we will face disappointment. Is there someone or something that you are turning to for approval? Make God first in your life and see your value through His eyes instead. Keep a journal or record of how making God first in your life changes you.

3. When was the last time you put on your "happy face" in order to keep up family appearances? In a moment of struggle, I recently commented to a friend that my family is not all that I want it to be, to which she responded, "Nobody's is." Friend, you are not alone if you have secrets in your family that you want to hide. Everybody does. An important thing to remember is that you can only take responsibility for your own actions and walk with the Lord. As a mom, it is our job to teach our children and be an example to our husband and family, but it is up to others to apply and maintain their personal walk with the Lord. Are you trying to "fix" faith and relationship issues between God and family members? You can't. But you *can* pray, and prayer changes things. Begin to journal your prayers for family members today so that you can have a record of how God works in each circumstance you cover in prayer.

4. As her marriage struggled and the writer attempted to fix her problems, she made the choice to abort—not just once, but twice. However, two poor choices added to her previous poor choices didn't make things any better. When we continue to stack sin upon sin to

fix our mistakes, we are creating a house of cards that will surely tumble. Have you ever experienced the spiral of sin? Describe it. Are you exhausted from the juggling act of trying to cover or make up for poor choices you may have made in your past, or possibly even in your present? Explain.

5. Friend, God is waiting to forgive you. Take your choices, the good and the bad, and give them all to Him. He is waiting to redeem them all and to give the peace and healing that you need. Turn to the last chapter in this book now to learn more about His plan to redeem every part of your life, both the good *and* the bad for His glory.

Chapter 5: Secret Struggles: A Birthmother's Perspective

"For 'you were like sheep going astray,' but now you have returned to the Shepherd and Overseer of your souls." 1 Peter 2:25

1. Many of us have been taught to live by the "Good Book," but somehow, when it comes to making every day real life application to the words found in this book, we tend to think that it is outdated and not relevant. 1 Peter 1:14-16 states, "As obedient children, do not conform to the evil desires you had when you lived in ignorance. But just as he who called you is holy, so be holy in all you do; for it is written: 'Be holy, because I am holy.'" As a believer, do you understand and pursue the call to live a life that is holy even in today's culture? What do you think it means to live a life that is "holy?" Do you feel that this is possible? Why or why not?

2. Daniel 2:22 says, "He reveals deep and hidden things; he knows what lies in darkness, and light dwells with him." Any time you are having to do something in secret it should be a good indicator that you might need to stop and evaluate your actions. Was there ever a time when you or someone you knew was living in secret sin while thinking

that no one would ever know? We often think that our sinful choices affect only ourselves, but the story of Achan's sin in Joshua 7 tells us otherwise. Read the passage and list the people that Achan's sin impacted. Can you think of a time when you made a sinful choice that obviously impacted others besides yourself? Was it worth the heartache that it caused to yourself and to others?

3. What about the red flags that the writer said should have been warning signs to turn her away from this dangerous relationship? She was willing to compromise her beliefs and entertain lifestyles and habits that she knew were not pleasing to God. Have you ever ignored red flags and taken a path you never meant to travel? It is not too late to turn around and head the other direction and pursue God.

4. Have you or someone you know gotten pregnant while they were unmarried? It is much more accepted by society now than in previous times, but it is still a difficult and frightening journey for most because of the uncertainties that come with parenting and providing for a child. While our current society is more accepting of sex before marriage, God has the same perspective on sex before marriage that He's always had. He is the same yesterday, today, and forever. That means that when He said in the beginning (yesterday) that sex was good between Adam and Eve, it still holds true for husbands and wives today that sex is a good thing within a married relationship. It also means that when He said in 1 Corinthians 6:1 (yesterday) to "Flee from sexual immorality . . . " that this also still applies today. It is so important to clarify that even though God may not be pleased with the actions that led to pregnancy if you are unwed and involved in sexual activity, He *is* pleased with the child that He created because *He* created it! How do I know? Because His word tells us that "Children are a blessing and a gift from the Lord" (Psalm 127:3 CEV). So, if that is what He said yesterday, then it is still true today in each circumstance. Never doubt it!

Chapter 5 Bonus: Adoption 101

Have you ever given much thought to adoption? I don't necessarily mean thought to adopting a child yourself but rather, thought to how you feel about the big picture of adoption. I would like for you to be educated on this rarely discussed subject, so read these thoughts carefully and apply in future conversations regarding adoption!

I would like for you to speak about adoption with different terminology. What if instead of "giving her baby away," you said, "She made an adoption plan for her baby." Just think how differently that sounds and even feels when you say it. Think of the difference in the intentions and the care that is given in the second statement. A mother is showing great care and concern for her baby when she prepares for her child by considering the life that she wants her baby to have and then spending time carefully and purposefully selecting a family that displays the unique qualities and abilities to provide that dream.

What about when someone suggests that the birth mother goes on with her life without a care? I hope you heard in the writer's story that she did care, very much in fact. An adoption placement is something that a mother grieves, much like an actual loss of life of a child. Hope can be found in knowing that one day, like the writer and her son, there may be an opportunity to be reunited and share a relationship again.

Do you realize that we are given several biblical examples of adoption in the Bible? Think of Moses, adopted by Pharaoh's daughter. His mother knew that it was not in Moses's best interests to stay and be raised in her home, so she placed him in God's hands and chose to let him go. The life and experiences that he had while growing up in Pharaoh's household prepared him to be the exact vessel that God needed to free the Israelites since he understood the culture. Moses could gain access to the country's leaders when he needed them. He had a very clear understanding of what it meant for a people that he loved to live in bondage. I think that we could all say that Moses thrived in life, in part due to his adoption experience.

There is also the example of Mordecai who adopted and raised his niece, Esther. This same Esther rose to the title of "Queen" in a nation where her people were to be subjected to annihilation had she not been exactly where she was for "such a time as this." Jesus Himself lived as the adopted Son of His earthly father, Joseph, and became the Savior of the world and Heir of all creation—not too shabby of a resume. Jesus's death on the cross also paved the way for *our* right to be called sons (and daughters!) of God, as we choose to accept the sacrifice that He made on our behalf to free us from slavery to sin. Through his sacrifice on the cross, we can now cry out "Abba, Father!"

Have you done this? Have you called on God to accept you as His child? If you answered no, or if you want more information about what that looks like, please turn now to the last chapter of this book to read more.

Chapter 6: Marriage, Ministry, and Porn

"We have escaped like a bird from the fowler's snare; the snare has been broken, and we have escaped. Our help is in the name of the Lord, the Maker of heaven and earth." Psalm 124:7-8

1. The writer noted that she felt that she had to live up to the world's portrayal of what sex should look like. Maybe you have also bought into the lie that you must live up to the images you see in pictures, movies, and on the Internet. It is important to recognize that your value involves so much more than your sex appeal or performance. Each day we should look in the mirror, and instead of focusing on our perceived flaws and imperfections, remind ourselves that no matter what we may have been told, we are God's workmanship and we are wonderfully made (Psalm 139).

2. The writer spoke of the emptiness of a relationship centered around fulfilling her husband's sexual demands. Satisfying sexual needs and having an intimate relationship are two different things. The Lord created us for companionship and intimacy, which involves engaging in emotional needs and a desire for personal communication. When true intimacy is lacking, it is possible to still feel empty regardless of how often we have sex with our partner. How would you describe your current relationship: fulfilling physically and emotionally, or lonely and empty? If you answered lonely and empty, have you discussed your feelings with your partner? If the answer is no, why not? Make a specific plan for when this conversation will take place.

3. Any object or activity—alcohol, golf, drugs, books, sexual relationships— can become an unhealthy outlet if used to run away from problems rather than facing them. Are you using unhealthy methods to cope with unmet needs and emotions, to run away from reality, or to be able to continue to function in a relationship?

4. Your partner may have a different type of addiction or other issues with anger that lead to physical, emotional, or verbal abuse. If you find yourself lying or making excuses to the people around you to cover for your partner's actions, or to protect his image or profession, this should be a red flag warning you of possible danger. Confide in a wise person that you trust to give you honest feedback and help you to safety.

5. Based on her description as a nurse, a mom, and the wife of a minister, most people would automatically rule the writer out as a candidate for the circumstances that she was dealing with and the services she has utilized to help her pull through. Never assume because of someone's education, job title, or income level that they have it all together. Please don't be too proud to ask for help, no matter what

your public role or image might be. Also don't assume that you won't qualify for certain types of help based on your income. There are many organizations in your community that are hoping and even praying that someone just like you will turn to them for help today. If they don't happen to have the resources you need, they are still likely to have referrals or provide contacts that will be invaluable to you. Remember that if you decide to remove yourself from an abusive situation, there will be a transitional stage where you may need temporary assistance with finances, emotional support, or other resources that exist. Allow yourself the grace to seek the resources that are available. Pray for guidance to find the right place and/or person for help.

6. In an abusive relationship, the victim may normalize issues in her mind by convincing herself that she is imagining things, or that things aren't as bad as they seem. She may tell herself that her abuser is simply having a bad day, or even that she deserves the treatment she's receiving because she has accepted false guilt. Nobody is perfect, but condemnation is not from Christ. In fact, He came to take the punishment for our sins so that we would be condemned no more! Jesus Christ is the perfect example of what true love really looks like: He died to protect us and to bring us freedom from eternal condemnation. In Christ, we can approach the throne of God boldly, with confidence in His grace toward us, His protection over us, and assurance of His love for us.

7. It is difficult for a victim to admit that she has allowed herself to be deceived or lured into an unhealthy relationship. It requires her to acknowledge that she has been manipulated emotionally, verbally, physically, or sexually. It may make her feel stupid or helpless, especially if she brought others who depend on her into the situation as well. Is there an unhealthy relationship in your life that you need to

acknowledge? Don't allow pride to hinder you from seeking the help and resources you need.

8. The writer referenced the "power and control" wheel. This is a tool which is often used to help women in abusive relationships see different behavioral traits used by an abusive partner to maintain power and control. If you have any questions about the relationship that you are in and whether someone's behavior might indicate that there is cause for concern that they are abusive or could become violent, view this resource. The wheel can be easily found online using a Google search.

9. The writer recognized God sustaining her emotionally as He spoke to her through nature, allowing her to see beauty in the world despite the everyday ugliness of her circumstances. Is God speaking to you in the middle of your circumstances as well? Write down any words that you think God may be speaking to you. Then grab a Bible concordance and look up every Scripture reference tied to that word and consider the context and the way it is used as you seek clarity in what God is speaking.

10. "Our family dynamic has changed . . . " Your journey will be a process and healing won't happen overnight. There will be issues that you will address that will require change along the way: change in expectations for relationships, change in the way you see yourself, change in your heart's desires, possibly changes in friends, jobs, and yes, it might even require a change of address. But through it all, I hope that change will come in the way you see, feel, hear, and value the presence of God in your life. He will be with you through the journey because He promises never to leave or forsake those who are His. Which leads me to the ask: are you His? If you want to know more about what this means, turn to the last chapter in this book now. No need to wait. This is probably the only book you will

ever read where the author instructs you to bypass the middle and go straight to the ending! The last chapter of this book is what the author of each of the chapters most wants you to hear anyway. So, don't delay, and turn there now friend.

Chapter 7: Longing for Home

"Jesus replied, 'Anyone who loves me will obey my teaching. My Father will love them, and we will come to them and make our home with them.'" John 14:23

1. Has God's plan for your life ever taken an unexpected turn? Maybe you chose to follow God down an unexpected path, believing that your obedience would lead to an easy path, only to find instead, that you've faced challenge after challenge. First Corinthians 15:58 says "Therefore, my dear brothers and sisters, stand firm. Let nothing move you. Always give yourselves fully to the work of the Lord, because you know that your labor in the Lord is not in vain." Do you believe that your efforts to walk in obedience will be rewarded? What keeps you from believing?

2. When faced with a life-threatening circumstance, the writer came face to face with core values that she professed to believe. She now had to decide if her actions were going to reflect what she said she believed, even if it meant dying. If you were observing your life from the outside, would you say that your actions and choices line up with what you say you believe? Would your faith endure to the point of death?

3. Sometimes other people won't be as excited as we are about the call that God has placed on our lives. "Am I now trying to win the approval of human beings, or of God? Or am I trying to please people? If I were still trying to please people, I would not be a servant of Christ" (Galatians 1:10). There will be times that we will

simply have to accept that there will be people who don't agree with the path that we take in our efforts to please Christ. Have you ever been discouraged by people who care and may even be believers but tried to keep you from following what you feel certain is God's call for you? Explain.

4. We will all face difficult seasons in life. I hope that in those moments, you, too, will experience the warmth of His presence there to comfort you. Psalm 18:39 says, "You armed me with strength for battle." As you walk through hardship, listen for His whispers that will comfort your soul. Watch for the small blessings, the little reminders that He is there, walking with you. Make a list today of the verses He has whispered or the blessings He has given to comfort you and reassure you of His presence.

5. Have you ever worked at a job that you felt was beneath you? Sometimes God allows these circumstances to teach us to have a servant's heart. If you are waiting for greater things to come your way, have patience, serve where you are, and learn about the Lord each step of the way. There are great lessons to be had in the "servant seasons" of life. Perhaps you could list a few things you've learned through serving.

6. "Home." That one word means something very different to every person. I recently saw a picture that included definitive sayings for the word home including, "a retreat from the world," "resting place," "haven," "where you will always feel loved," "a sanctuary," "full of love." These sayings are just the *beginning* of the list of many wonderful descriptions of our heavenly home. Don't miss it, this heavenly home. There is a room there, just for you! Read the last chapter of this book to find out more about how you can spend eternity in this home with Christ!

Chapter 8: Depression, Suicide, and Healing Mercy

"The Spirit of the Sovereign LORD is on me, because the LORD has anointed me to proclaim good news to the poor. He has sent me to bind up the brokenhearted, to proclaim freedom for the captives and release from darkness for the prisoners . . ." Isaiah 61:1

1. "Satan finds loopholes . . . cracks . . . vulnerable areas . . . " the writer stated. We *all* have cracks and vulnerable areas that Satan will seek to use to attack us in our weakest moment so we need to be prepared. Prepared doesn't mean scared because even though he may attack, he does not have the power to overcome those who belong to Christ. Has Satan attacked you recently? Think about the area of weakness that he targeted. How can you make that area of weakness stronger? Ask God to help you overcome that area of weakness and then memorize a few verses that speak specifically to it so that when Satan tries to attack you in the future, you can quickly refute him with God's truth!

2. Has Satan ever caused you to see yourself in a way that wasn't true? Maybe he's told you that you are not pretty enough or stylish enough, or that you simply aren't beautiful enough. When God beholds you, He sees you as His masterpiece, created by His very own hands! Even more than outer beauty, God sees your heart. He sees your inner beauty, and 1 Peter 3:34 says that your inner beauty is of great worth in God's sight. Name something beautiful about yourself right now, and then believe it to be true!

3. Have you ever wished you could just start over in life? In his book *If*, author Mark Batterson likens the changes we need to make in our thought processes to what takes place in the reset process for a phone.

5   Batterson, Mark. *If: Trading Your If Only Regrets for God's What If Possibilities* (United States: Baker Publishing Group, 2016), 62-63.

He said that as a new creation in Christ we don't need a "soft reset" to change the way we operate, but rather a "hard reset" that completely wipes the "old data" or way of thinking so that you don't keep making the same poor choices and wishing you could start all over again. Maybe you don't really need to start over after all. Maybe you just need to adopt a new way of thinking about things.[6] Romans 12:2 states "Do not conform to the pattern of this world, but be transformed by the renewing of your mind . . ." Think about issues related to poor choices you may have made in the past and look for verses that address God's thoughts on those issues. Allow those verses to reset your thinking and help shape your future choices.

4. If you look at the actual definition of the word purge, you might be surprised to find that in one sense it can have a healthy connotation. *Purge* is defined by Google as "rid (someone or something) of an unwanted quality, condition, or feeling." Consider what thoughts or emotions you might need to purge from your heart so that you can have a healthier outlook. List a few and then pray over that list.

5. 1 Corinthians 13:12 "For now we see only a reflection as in a mirror; then we shall see face to face. Now I know in part; then I shall know fully, even as I am fully known." Do you have this longing to be fully known? There is one who knows you far beyond what is only seen from the outside and He loves you anyway. If you want to experience a relationship like this turn to the final chapter of this book to learn more.

Chapter 8: Bonus

In our society today, suicide is more common than ever before. In fact, in 2017 it was the tenth leading cause of death in the U.S., with an average of 129 suicides per day. People are tired, overwhelmed, and constantly barraged

6   https://afsp.org

with the hardships and sadness of events that surround them in this world to the point that they begin to feel hopeless and are simply looking for a way to escape. Let me reassure you that thoughts like these signal a need for help. If you are seriously considering taking your life—and by that I mean that you are researching effective ways that you might do it, writing good-bye letters to family and friends in your mind or actually on paper, or engaging in other similar activities, seek help. Tell your family, talk to a pastor or a close friend (preferably an adult), or find a Christian counselor to help you. Because they care about you, your family or those closest to you may want to attend counseling with you. Be honest about your thoughts so that they can offer the help you need.

Most importantly, know that God hasn't forgotten you. He sees you in your weakest moments and He loves you no matter what. In Mark 5, Jesus came to the country of the Gerasene where a man named Legion lived among the tombs crying out night and day and cutting himself with stones. (Yes, cutting is in the Bible and the heart wrenching pain and tears that accompany such activities of self-inflicted harm is something that Jesus is very familiar with.) Jesus commanded the demons to leave the man and sent them into a nearby herd of pigs who then rushed into the sea and drowned. As people tend to do when unusual activity takes place, they came rushing to see what had just happened. What they saw was the man they knew as tormented sitting calmly, clothed, and in his right mind.

Here is where I want you to lean in. While the man wanted to leave his surroundings behind and go to be with Jesus, Jesus did not permit it. In fact, Jesus had a job for him to do. He said, 1) "Go home to your own people"; 2) "Tell them how much the Lord has done for you"; 3) [tell them] "how he has had mercy on you" (Mark 5:19).

No matter how distraught or tormented you may be, time with Jesus can cast a spirit of wailing and self-inflicted harm away. Until He calls you to come and be with Him, He intends for you to stay on this earth and complete your

God-given assignment here. The first step is to get your head on straight. Find godly friends and counsel that will encourage you as you diligently make time to spend with Jesus and experience His love for you. Allow Him to calm your spirit and speak to the demons that haunt you. Jesus wants you to experience Him in such a way that your life is forever changed, so that just like Legion, you will become one who causes people to marvel at the work He has done in your life. No matter how badly you may want to leave it all behind and just be with Him, God isn't finished with you yet. He is bigger than anything that has control over your mind or your life. Turn to Him today.

Chapter 9: He Gives and Takes Away

"'The Lord gave and the Lord has taken away; may the name of the Lord be praised.' In all this, Job did not sin by charging God with wrongdoing." Job 1:21-22

1. The writer noted that the news of her first pregnancy did not come in the place or the way that she had always pictured. Maybe it wasn't an unplanned pregnancy that caught you off guard, but instead, your marriage hasn't turned out like you thought it would, or your career path took a different turn than you expected. Or maybe it *was* an unplanned pregnancy that changed the course of your life. Whatever it may have been, how did you deal with your less than ideal situation? Have you taken it to God and allowed Him to bring beauty from the ashes?

2. Have you ever "abandoned God?" The wonderful news is that even when we abandon Him, He never abandons us. Peter provides a perfect example of one who abandoned Christ but who was later redeemed and used by God to serve in His kingdom in powerful ways. 1 John 1:9 says, "If we confess our sins, he is faithful and just and will forgive us our sins and purify us from all unrighteousness." Don't

wait another minute to let His faithfulness restore your relationship with Him so that you can be about the wonderful works that He has in store for you to do!

3. Relationship with God is about so much more than being "raised as a church girl." How would you classify your own relationship with God? Is it really a relationship built on living your life with and for Him, or is your Christian experience more about a religious title that you wear or a building that you go to?

4. God often works in ways that we simply don't understand. If you've ever experienced failure and saw it as nothing but your ruin, I would encourage you to look to an example like Moses. Killing an Egyptian in an outburst of anger prompted Moses to flee from Egypt and spend 40 years in the desert leading and caring for herds of sheep. God used this time as training to prepare Moses to lead the Israelites out of slavery (Genesis 2:12;15; 3:10). Stories of people like Moses remind us that God can take our worst mistake and redeem it to bring growth to us and glory to Himself. What failure would you most like to turn over to God today?

5. Has there ever been a circumstance in your own life where you've asked God, "Why can't I get over this?" What was His response to you? How would it change your perspective on healing and God's goodness toward you if you considered approaching your situation from the viewpoint that getting over everything isn't always the answer?

6. Have you ever reached the end of your rope? Where did you turn? If it was to anything other than Christ, it may have worked for a minute, but I can assure you that it won't fill the longings of your heart. The only thing that fixes the "end" is a new beginning with God leading the way. Today is the today. What is holding you back from your new beginning in Him? If you want to know more about how to take that step turn to the last chapter of this book now.

Chapter 10: Moments That Define Us

"For God speaks once, and even twice, yet no one notices it [including you, Job].
In a dream, a vision of the night [one may hear God's voice], when deep sleep
falls on men while slumbering upon the bed, then He opens the ears of men
and seals their instruction . . . " Job 33:14-16 (AMP)

1. While the writer didn't recognize her life-defining moment at the time it occurred, in hindsight she could see it as she looked at the big picture. Do you recognize a moment in your life that made a major impact on you? Has it defined aspects of the rest of your life and who you determined to become? If so, would you consider this to be a good thing and something that you are at peace with or is it something you wrestle with within yourself or that perhaps you are still wrestling out with God?

2. Do you believe that God still speaks? If so, has He ever spoken to you and what did He sound like? To the prophet Elijah His voice sounded like a whisper; to Job He was a dream; to Moses He was a burning bush; to the Israelites He was a cloud by day and a consuming fire by night. Write down what He said when He spoke to you. Did it change anything about your life, your circumstances, or your perspective about a situation?

3. There will be times in your life when you will be certain that you heard God speak to you about something, but it may not come to pass immediately. This could lead you to feel that maybe you were mistaken in thinking you heard God's voice. But sometimes God is simply planting a thought or an idea as a seed in your heart that needs time before it is ready to bear fruit. The writer mentioned that God was faithful to tell her family what they needed to know when they needed to know it. Recognize His voice and discern His presence so that you can stand firm and wait for His Words to come to pass in

His time and in His way. If you are comfortable, share something He spoke to you that you are waiting to see unfold.

4. The writer had to come to understand at one point in her journey that it wasn't about figuring out the *whys* of the situation or what was *wrong* with her son. Let me encourage you as well that you may never know "why" you have found yourself in the situation that you are in, or what went wrong to get you there. You may never know what is "wrong" with you or with others who are presenting challenges to you in the moment. Like the writer, rest in knowing that these are things that you don't have to know because God knows it all! Simply trust Him each day to take care of you right where you are and just as you are. He will never disappoint you. What are some verses in the Bible that can assure you of this? Jot them in your journal or in the margins on this page.

5. What challenge is it that you are facing in the moment? What positive aspect of the situation can you choose to focus on? Ecclesiastes 7:14 says it all too well: "Enjoy prosperity while you can, but when hard times strike, realize that both come from God. Remember that nothing is certain in this life." There is no promise of tomorrow. Only God knows the number of days ordained for you and me. He is the One you will meet face to face at the end of those days. If you want to know how you can be prepared whether tomorrow holds life or death in its hands, turn now to the last chapter of this book to learn more.

About the Author

Beth Grisham is a wife, mother, and ministry leader whose greatest passion is studying the Word of God to find simple truths which are often overlooked and teaching them to others in a way that brings insight and application to the details of everyday life.

A graduate of the University of North Alabama, Beth obtained a Bachelor of Science in Communications. However, her greatest education came after she completed college and became a mother to her six children who now range from ages fourteen to twenty-seven.

Although Beth prayed to receive Christ at age eighteen, it wasn't until the loss of her third child when she was twenty-six that she developed a personal relationship with Christ and dove headlong into His Word. Her loss was the beginning of a whole new way of life, and a totally different perspective about what is most important in this world. It's often stated that your greatest ministry will come from your greatest pain, and that has certainly proven itself true in Beth's life. She considers motherhood and the raising up of a next generation of Christ followers to be the greatest blessing she will ever have and her greatest opportunity to make a Kingdom impact on the world that we live in.

Beth lives in North Alabama with her husband Packy and their two youngest children who still reside at home.

For more information about

Beth Grisham
and
Seeds of Perspective
please visit:

SmallBeginnings.blog

For more information about
AMBASSADOR INTERNATIONAL
please visit:

www.ambassador-international.com
@AmbassadorIntl
www.facebook.com/AmbassadorIntl

*If you enjoyed this book, please consider leaving us a review on
Amazon, Goodreads, or our website.*

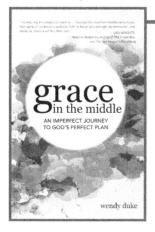

Grace in the Middle is a memoir recounting one young couple's struggle to hold on to an unraveling faith during the greatest crisis of their lives. Heartbreaking, triumphant, and funny in just the right places, this inspiring story is an authentic reflection on battling and overcoming physical illness and disability, resisting the dark doubts that plague us in the midst of tragedy, and trusting the faithfulness of God through the deep twists and turns of life.

Vanna Nguyen had escaped a war-ravaged Vietnam to make a life in America. Life seemed good and was finally settling down as Vanna planned a graduation party for her daughter Queena. But one phone call completely derailed those plans and sent Vanna and her daughters down a road that they had never dreamed they would travel. The Bloomingdale Library Attack Survivor made a name for herself, but in a way no mother would ever want. Read about two women from the same family who fought against all odds to "make beauty from ashes."

One night can change everything. Abby Banks put her healthy, happy infant son to sleep, but when she awoke the next morning, she felt as though she was living a nightmare. Her son, Wyatt, was paralyzed. In an instant, all her hopes and dreams for him were wiped away. As she struggled to come to grips with her son's devastating diagnosis and difficult rehabilitation, she found true hope in making a simple choice, a choice to love anyway—to love her son, the life she didn't plan, and the God of hope, Who is faithful even when the healing doesn't come.

Made in the USA
Coppell, TX
10 September 2022

82950954R00095